Money Saving Home Repair Guide

Gary Paulsen

Ideals Publishing Corp.
Milwaukee, Wisconsin

Table of Contents

ISBN 0-8249-6100-5

Copyright © 1981 by Ideals Publishing Corporation

All rights reserved. This book or parts thereof, may not be reproduced in any form without permission of the copyright owners. Printed and bound in the United States of America. Published simultaneously in Canada.

Published by Ideals Publishing Corporation
11315 Watertown Plank Road
Milwaukee, Wisconsin 53226

Editor, David Schansberg

Cover designed by David Schansberg. Materials courtesy of Elm Grove Ace Hardware.

Cover photo by Jerry Koser

⌂ SUCCESSFUL
HOME IMPROVEMENT SERIES

Bathroom Planning and Remodeling
Kitchen Planning and Remodeling
Space Saving Shelves and Built-ins
Finishing Off Additional Rooms
Finding and Fixing the Older Home
Money Saving Home Repair Guide
Homeowner's Guide to Tools
Homeowner's Guide to Electrical Wiring
Homeowner's Guide to Plumbing
Homeowner's Guide to Roofing and Siding
Homeowner's Guide to Fireplaces
Home Plans for the '80s
How to Build Your Own Home

Avoiding Repair Through Maintenance

Perhaps the greatest irony in any discussion of home repair—for any area of the home—is that the best home repair is the one you didn't have to make. Barring natural disasters and accidents, a major portion of all home repairs could have been prevented.

Most problems around the home which require repair or replacement are caused by sheer neglect. This neglect is not purposeful. It often arises from ignorance more than anything else.

Consider a small leak in a roof. It can be easily fixed, usually with a bit of tar or mastic. The job can take less than five minutes and cost under a dollar. But if the leak is allowed to develop and grow, the ensuing damp-damage to the attic and roof trusses can be nearly catastrophic. It's quite possible that a few months neglect can cause major roof damage over an extended period. If the rot goes into the rafters it might well require roof replacement, which is virtually as expensive as building new.

So before getting down to specific repairs, here is a general discussion on prevention of major repairs.

The way the house "feels" to you, the person who has to live in it, can have a measurable effect on the when and/or how of home repair.

A home heating system that is ill designed for your specific needs (for instance, inadequate in those areas where you want heat, or too much for comfort) can breed a kind of mental distaste—a subtle almost-anger that can cause repair problems because you may overload the system working it too hard, or imbalance it to try to make it fit your needs, or neglect the whole thing because in a hidden part of your mind you resent it. If some part of the house does not suit your needs, think about changing it, replacing it or remodeling it, lest it become a repair problem down the road.

Maintenance

Usually, when presenting methods of repair prevention, the term *maintenance* is brought in. And to be sure, a thorough program of maintenance can prevent most problems.

In home maintenance there is a tendency to hit a superficial level and let it go. The classic illustration of this tendency to skip over important items is the forced air heating system. Each late summer or fall most people replace the input air filters. Then they set their thermostats and forget the heating system for the rest of the winter.

While it is true that replacing the filters is vital because it can save money in heating bills and ease the work of the blower, it is only the tip of the iceberg when it comes to preventive maintenance. True heating system maintenance should take an entire day, cover not just the filters but the blower motor, duct system, and chimney.

The thing to remember is that P.M. (preventive maintenance), to be effective, must be comprehensive and done in sufficient detail to catch any and all trouble spots in the house. Keeping an accurate record of maintenance on your home can mean large savings in time, money and headaches. With home prices and all associated costs continually rising, a good maintenance system could easily save thousands of dollars.

Don't just run out and get a clipboard and tablet and scribble a blurb about the heater now and again. Be thorough. Break the house down into its various systems. A basic starting list of the different systems to record follows. It is only an example. If you have other systems be sure to add them; better too many than not enough.

- Main house
- Heating and air-conditioning system
- Plumbing system
- Roof and attic
- Electrical system
- Exterior wall (and siding)
- Windows (including storms and screens) and doors (including storms and screens)
- Interior walls and ceilings
- Floors (and floor covering) which can also include stairways
- Foundation and basement which includes waterproofing, and the floor joists overhead if they are visible
- Appliances including dishwasher, clothes washer and drier, kitchen range, ovens (including microwave) and all other major appliances in the home
- Supplementary, to include any and all systems or structures not already covered

It is, as might be expected, a substantial amount of work to formulate accurate maintenance records but once they are done the work eases out and the jobs take on order.

For the Main House record or log, you simply list the other systems to maintain order, and keep a running tally of dates checked, as per the sample below:

Main House		
Item Checked	*Date*	*Remarks*
Heating system	Jan.	Filter changed.
Plumbing system	Feb.	Damp around commode (see plumbing log for details).
Roof and Attic	Mar.	Small leak in N/W corner (see roof log for details).

And so on. Just a way to minimize the confusion. It is in getting down to the individual lists where comprehensiveness pays off. Following are several suggested logs and their application—again, shown as an example only. Don't limit yourself. Pay close attention to manufacturer's information booklets, especially for appliances and heating or air-conditioning systems. Often they furnish a complete maintenance list which you simply have to copy. And finally, remember that the main thrust of maintenance records is to stop expensive repairs before they happen, so it's better to be too picky than to miss something.

Heating System		
Item Checked	*Date*	*Remarks*
Filter	Aug.	Put in new filter.
Ducting	Aug.	Cleaned dust and cobwebs.
Motor	Sept.	Oiled bearings.
Burners	Sept.	O.K.
Pilot system	Sept.	O.K.
Pipes (for hot water)	Sept.	Slight dampness; keep watching.
Boiler (hot water)	Sept.	O.K.

And so forth. The important part of this list is to keep a running maintenance comment so that if something starts to go bad it will show. For example, the dampness around the pipes in the hot water system may simply be condensation that will dry off. But it also might be a pinpoint leak which if watched could be stopped before it develops further.

Write everything down whether or not it seems important at the time. In the heating system log, for example, the cleaning of dust and cobwebs from around the ducts is noted not simply because it eliminates a fire danger but by noting the date it is possible to see how fast dust accumulates and determine if your filter should be changed more frequently.

Electrical System		
Item Checked	*Date*	*Remarks*
Visible wiring (in basement, etc.)		Inspected for fraying, burned spots.
Circuit breaker box (or fuse box)		Dirt, dust, burned spots.
Outlets and switches		Clean and working properly.
Light fixtures		Replace burned out bulbs, check wires, clean.
Power lines into house		Clear of branches and drains.
Loading		Check any circuit that pops breakers or blows fuses.

All electrical items should be considered potentially dangerous. For that reason any inspection of electrical wires should be done as carefully as possible, paying close attention to safety logic and rules laid down in the chapter on electrical repairs. If you aren't comfortable enough with electrical work to do a good job, stay away from it.

Roof and Gutters		
Item Checked	*Date*	*Remarks*
Visible roof		Clean, not decomposing
Attic		No rot, no dampness, good insulation
Gutters		Clear, open, not rusted or jammed
Soffit; eaves		No rot, loose or hanging soffit material
Branches		Not scraping through roofing material

Frequency of the checks is not as critical as being sure they get done. Also, it varies greatly with area, weather conditions, the type of dwelling, and material used in construction. Checking the roof once a year, for example, right before bad winter or rainy weather, is probably more than ample to catch any and all problems. The floor only needs a check every year or so. Running one general maintenance check each year will probably suffice; it is certainly more than many home dwellers do. By cycling the checks around the year, it is possible to further reduce the labor to one small inspection each month. Little enough work if it prevents calling the contractor.

Aging

Houses begin to get old the minute they're finished and moved into. With the rapid workmanship and the still-green wood going into many houses due to increased demand, aging problems in houses are understandable.

The problems covered in this chapter are caused by the natural aging process, due to all the materials getting older and the house settling over time.

Sagging

A general settling over the years is to be expected and presents no real problem. Some tiny cracks will appear in the plaster. Now and then you'll hear a creak, and some lines that should have been straight will have a slight curve. Nothing really bad will happen. That's just normal aging, and isn't all that important.

But now and then a piece of wood will let go, or the sagging of a house will cause the doors to work poorly or jam the windows. This is when aging becomes a hazard and repair is necessary.

The first step is to locate the center of the sag. That is not as difficult as it sounds. You go into the basement or crawlspace beneath the point where you first noticed the sag and make a visual inspection. If a door frame upstairs, for instance, has been getting tighter and tighter to work, you go into the basement under that point and study the overhead.

The point of sag will show, visually, as the low point in a curve.

The trick is to get it to go back up, and again, it's really a very simple process. Rent a five-ton jack from the nearest rental agency, cut a 4 x 4-inch post off to use as a jacking member, and take a second piece to spread the load. Then jack the house back up, as illustrated.

Go very slowly, just a hair at a time, to give all the boards time to catch up with this reverse movement. Don't overdo it. The house will move easily, perhaps too easily, and there is a tendency to overcompensate.

When you have between half an inch and an inch of movement, stop! Leave everything as it is and go upstairs to see that the door or windows are working properly again. If so, don't go any further, because you will go too far and cause structural problems the other way. Be satisfied with what you've achieved.

Leave the jack holding the sagging section up, and build a support. Using 4 x 4-inch posts, build a post-and-support-beam to hold the adjusted section up.

This post should rest on cement. If the basement has a cement floor, cut the vertical posts to rest on the cement and that will do it.

If the floor is earth, which might be the case in an older home, buy two small solid slab-blocks measuring 8 x 16 x 4 inches thick and use them for mini-footings for the vertical supports. Just put the post so it hits in the middle of the block on each end, and the two will hold up each end of the support beam.

With the beam in place, release the jack so the weight comes down on the support structure. Then go upstairs to see if the doors work properly.

If the corrected surface comes down too much, jack it back up and shim above the posts with shimming shingles between the post and support.

If you intend to occupy the area beneath the sag, it

Jack the house up just enough to remove the sag.

is necessary to place the posts so they will be out of the way. One can go flush against the wall, but the other must be in the proposed room. If this is the case, place it either centrally, or where you propose putting a corner at some future date. This will save moving it later.

If the sag is in a corner of the house, which is common in soft-soiled areas, the post support system is not necessary. Jack the corner up as with the central sag, but then simply jam shimming shingles back between the sill plate (the board that the floor joists are nailed to) and the top of the foundation wall. Pound the shingles in with a hammer, spaced every three or four inches, to ensure an even distribution of weight.

Release the jack slowly, and check to make sure the problems are gone. Many or most older homes are not adequately insulated, if at all. This problem is most evident where the house meets the foundation and it is not uncommon to find actual air-gaps between the sill plate and the foundation wall.

Go around and pack fiberglass insulation into the crack between the sill plate and the foundation; jam it in with a screwdriver or chisel and even hammer it a bit to make it tight.

Finally, look above the sill plate between the floor joists. If there isn't any insulation, cut squares and put them up between the joists as illustrated.

This does not count as an actual repair, but if you are down there anyway it can save some pretty good chunks on the heating bill.

The biggest danger in correcting a sag is not distributing the load over a wide enough area, so use a long 4 x 4 across the top. Don't, under any circumstances, jack it back up over an inch.

Shrinkage

Another problem due to aging is shrinkage. As wood becomes old and dries out, it shrinks.

This causes noises, creaks, and a general opening of seams that might be considered unsightly. It will be especially noticeable in molding corners on the floor or ceiling, and in the finished carpentry work of exposed box beams and hairline cracks in plaster or drywall seams.

You can't make the wood return to its original size, but you can compensate for the shrinkage to make it look better.

First, if the shrinkage has caused a pulling apart of two boards, use a buffer board and try pounding them back together. This form of repair would work in such cases as a top door casing that lifts up and off the two vertical trim boards. Just tap it back down, not with massive blows but firm taps, and a buffer board between so the trim board doesn't get damaged by the hammer. This method would also

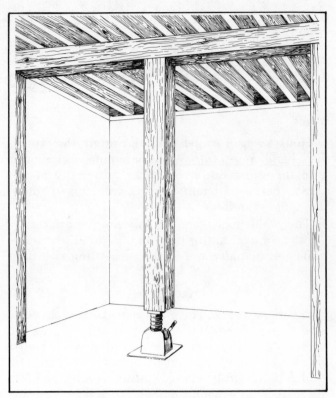

When the house is jacked on the 4 x 4 beam, put in two vertical supports to take the weight; then remove the jack.

work on an outside corner of molding, where the two mitered boards have moved apart, leaving a crack. Once again, just firmly tap them back together.

On inside corners, or in other cases where hammering can't bring the boards back together, the repair is slightly more involved.

Wear rubber gloves and work wood filler into the crack with your thumb. Using premixed, precolored wood filler will make the job easier. When the crack is filled, stain or paint to match if necessary. Be sure to work the filler completely back into the crack with your finger or thumb. If it only seals across the surface and does not achieve any depth, it will crack open later.

Door shrinkage problems will be covered in the chapter on doors, but vertically sliding windows present a particular problem when they become smaller. From left to right, the only effect is that they are slightly easier to slide up and down. But the shrinkage affecting them and allowing them to move back and forth can also cause them to wobble in the wind as well as let too much cold in and heat out.

To cure this, you do nothing to the window itself. Instead, inspect the window and you will notice that on wooden windows there is a strip that goes up the side of the casing so the window can slide; it is simply nailed in with finishing nails.

Using a screwdriver and a hammer, carefully

Drive the shingles in straight and hard. When they have moved the house up enough, cut them off flush with the wall and insulate the sill plate as shown.

Drive the fiberglass into the sill plate seam as hard as you can. Cut the insulation a little bigger than the space between the joists in order to stop all air leaks.

remove the slider strip, poke out the nails, and renail it back against the window so that it is snug the full vertical distance. This will "tighten" up the whole assembly and minimize the problems caused by aging.

The same aging-shrinkage sometimes causes the glass to be loose in the wooden-stopped windows—or in the old routed mullion kind. Repair procedures are essentially the same. Pull up the stops carefully, one at a time, and move them closer to the glass and renail. Use a piece of cardboard or fiberboard to protect the glass from the hammer. If you do not feel up to pulling all the stops, and it is only a small wobble in the glass, you might try a thin, pressured-in bead of caulking—all around the glass. Just squirt it in between the glass and then stop, being careful not to slop over.

Rot

The most critical structural problem found in older homes is rot, sometimes known as dry rot.

It will be found primarily in attics and basements, although it can show up anywhere. It starts with a blackening of the wood which eventually leads to the wood literally rotting and falling to pieces. To test for rot, probe and poke the wood with your screwdriver. Soft, easy-to-penetrate spots mean trouble, as does easy splintering.

If your house has rot, and the rot is advanced and in structural areas such as rafters or floor joists, there is little you can do except replace the rotted member. This is exactly as difficult and messy as it sounds, not at all something for the weekend do-it-yourselfer. The old member has to be ripped out, a new one cut and put in.

If, however, the rot is not greatly advanced and is present only in a single rafter or two, or maybe one floor joist, it is possible to repair it without undue hardship.

First, leave the rotted member in place. Clean it well with a wire brush. When it is thoroughly clean rub it well, with hard pressure, with handfuls of table salt. Rub the salt in thoroughly, so it works back into the grain of the rotted area.

The salt will not reverse the rotting, indeed it does little but arrest the problem. After you have salted liberally, sandwich the rotted board with two new, good ones, nailed from both sides with 16d nails on 8-inch or 10-inch centers. The repair should hold for a long time.

The most important aspect of repairing rot is not the job you are currently working on, but preventing problems that may develop in the future. If you have rot problems now, you had best establish a good maintenance program to stop future rot. Check all the structural members, and if rot has started—or even if it hasn't—rub liberally with salt, so that it has been thoroughly worked back into the grain.

Remember when dealing with rot that panic is a great danger. Just because there's a touch of rot here and there doesn't mean the house is going to cave in. But it does mean that you will have to pay attention to steady maintenance.

Foundations

Foundations signify one of the paradoxes of home owning—you see them the least, and they often matter the most.

Of course, as far as anything actually damaging the foundation of a house, the odds are relatively low. A hole is dug, cement or blocks are put down, the house is constructed, and that's the last you hear of it—or should.

Unfortunately many of the problems with foundations do not show up for years, and then they can be absolutely miserable.

Two of the most common will be examined, along with repair methods, but first a general word about difficulties with this type of work.

Everything to do with foundation repair is heavy, dirty, back-breaking work. If any of those descriptions throw you off, it might be best to bypass the work yourself and call in a contractor. In either case, be careful of quick fixes or shortcut jobs offered by self-proclaimed professional foundation men. The quick cures to foundation problems rarely work.

A trouble that isn't a trouble is the famous hairline crack in the foundation. It scares many home buyers or owners, but actually does little damage. It's usually only a normal function of curing cement or settling loads. If it bothers you, rub a bit of pre-mixed cement in the crack with your thumb and forget it. Here are the two major problems.

Basement Water

By far the most common ailment with foundations is water seepage through the walls into the basement, especially in the spring. It is caused by shoddy workmanship in initial construction of the home. The foundation wasn't waterproofed correctly with plaster and/or regular type tar, and adequate drainage (either with drain tube or drain tiles) was not provided.

It can cost you the use of half your house, cause the wood to rot faster and warp wildly because the humidity has increased so much, and generally be a pain for as long as you own the home.

Unfortunately, if such damage is present, there is absolutely *no* shortcut or easy way to correct the problem. Repair is hard, miserable work and is usually quite expensive.

If leakage is a problem, the only way to properly fix it is to dig down around the foundation of the house, all the way to the footing and start from scratch.

First, using premix, it is necessary to plaster the wall if it is made of block. Mix the mud so it's fairly sticky and a shade runny, and apply it with broad strokes and a wide, flat trowel. Plaster it an inch thick from the footing to ground level and all around wherever the earth meets the foundation. It doesn't matter how it looks, just so it's thick and bonds well to the blocks. After some practice you will find plastering relatively simple, but dirty.

Once the plaster coat is set, which takes a day or two, coat it well with foundation tar. Again, apply a very thick coat. Let the tar set for another day or two, and if the house is on a hill install a drain tube all around the footing with the two ends coming out the shallow or exposed end of footing. This allows

There are no shortcuts to proper waterproofing. Cover the entire surface with plastic and tar very carefully. One leak ruins it all.

the water to drain off before it gets into the house.

If you have a concrete foundation of poured cement the process is exactly the same except that you do not plaster with cement. It is already effectively "plastered" when it is poured. But you still must tar thickly, and put in the drain tube if the house is on a grade so it will have adequate drainage.

Because the repair is such a mess, reevaluate the problem before beginning the work.

First, check to be sure the water coming in is from seepage and not merely a small stream or something hitting the back of the house, in which case it could be diverted to stop the problem.

Second, can you live with the seepage? Seriously, if it isn't excessive, if it's merely a dampness, perhaps the problem isn't worth the work and expense of repairing it. If a drain can handle it well, or an automatic sump-pump feeding into a drain, it might be best to avoid the whole mess of repairing and live with the problem.

Large Foundation Cracks

Less common, but still enough of a difficulty to be worthy of mention, are large cracks in foundations, whether block or poured cement. These cracks are more important for what they might mean than what they are.

Before considering repair, find the reason for the crack. If it is an inch or more at the top, it needs immediate repair. Curing cement rarely cracks very

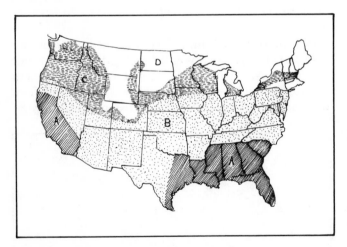

Termite susceptibility by geographic area.
A. *Region I (including Hawaii): termite protection required.*
B. *Region II: termite protection generally required, although specific areas are sometimes exempted.*
C. *Region III: termite protection usually not required, except for specific local areas.*
D. *Region IV (including Alaska): termite protection not required.*
Map courtesy of U.S. Department of Housing and Urban Development

wide; if it is wide enough to see all the way through, it probably means excessive settling in one corner because of inadequate footing surface.

Repairing of the crack is simple. Mix up a very dry, almost crumbly, mixture of premixed cement and pack it, literally, into the crack. Dry cement cures stronger than wet, but more important it tends to slightly expand and fill the crack.

Really pound it in there, push it back in, and let it cure several days before painting or covering with siding.

The secondary effects are not as easy to stop. If the crack holds and stays full, fine. But if the crack is caused by settling that is still occurring the crack will reappear in a few months. Watch it very closely and when it opens to a quarter inch or so repack it with a new dry-mixture of cement. If it just keeps expanding for years it could mean that the corner of the house is on a spring or some sort of slip rock (very rare), and it will be necessary to dig down and refoot the foundation; (a massive repair and best left to a contractor.)

Termites

Estimates show that termites cause close to $350 million of damage every year, although termite invasion can be recognized and caught at an early enough stage to prevent expensive repairs.

The first areas to check for termite damage are earth-filled areas covered by concrete, such as steps, porches, or a landscape planter. From these areas termites can spread out to nearby wood. They then crawl upward through openings in slab or foundation walls; a crack as thin as a sheet of paper can admit termites. To cross exposed areas they build mud tunnels that are easily identified, usually spanning wood joists or sills. They also leave trails of sawdust. Check the entire perimeter of your house for these tunnels or sawdust piles.

Inspection for termites is usually best carried out from below. Probe exposed wood parts with your screwdriver. If the point penetrates more than is normal, it may indicate termites. Where possible, remove any wood in contact with the ground, to deprive termites access to your house.

Other protective measures include:
• adequate drainage
• adequate ventilation
• proper flashing
• removal of all stumps, roots, or other wood debris
• clearance between ground surfaces and lumber

Before resorting to an exterminator, try a commercial termite killer. Also replace outdoor wood with treated wood whenever possible. Add soil poison to porch slabs, planter boxes, and partially-veneered sections.

Floors

Because there are so many different kinds of floors and floor coverings, there is no single common base for problem solving. Each floor is unique and has its own set of problems, and has to be fixed in its own way.

Hardwood Floors

Becoming less predominant, good hardwood floors are now found only in expensive new homes and older dwellings. They are beautiful, and worth preserving, and for that reason a good maintenance system is essential. Problems with hardwood floors are almost all due to aging.

Squeaking Floor Generally caused by shrinkage and a slight pulling out of the nails, a squeaking hardwood floor is relatively easy to fix. First, try coating the floor with a thin, *good* floor oil, the kind that soaks in. Usually this will work down into the cracks and make the wood swell back toward its normal size, which in turn "tightens" the floor and stops the squeaking. If the squeak persists, try pounding the floor down, using a heavy hammer and buffer board, at the point of the squeak and out around in ever-increasing circles. If that does not work, and it probably will, find the floor joist nearest to the squeak and nail the two or three boards down that seem to be squeaking. Be sure to nail at the seams, to spread the boards a bit and further jam them tighter together. Use 8d finishing nails, and sink the heads in ⅛ inch. Then fill with precolored filler stick.

Lifting Boards Over the decades hardwood flooring tends to lift as it shrinks and the house settles. Standing back, with your face lowered, you can actually see that some of the boards are higher than others. Use a buffer board and heavy hammer, and with firm blows tap the floor back down where it seems to have risen. Most of the boards will stay down, but for those places where they come back up, nail in the seams to joists with 8d finishing nails, sinking the nails ⅛ inch and filling with precolored filler stick.

Tipped or Canted Boards Now and then, due to water damage or a faulty piece of wood, a floor board will appear to warp, twist or turn one edge up—or more correctly, try to turn an edge up although the next board will hold it down. First try nailing on the seam, pulling the high side down into a floor joist. This will usually work; if you coat the

nail with glue and use a 10d finishing nail for extra length, the board will stay down. If the board does not stay down, try taking a really damp towel and a hot iron and steam-iron the warped part of the board for ten or fifteen minutes, really working the steam down into the crack. This usually softens the wood enough so that even the most stubborn board will stay down.

Finish Repair There are many things which can go wrong with the finish on a hardwood floor, everything from puppy stains to sun-baking where light comes through the window and cooks the floor.

Basically, however, the repair method is the same whether it is a big area or a small one. The bad finish has to come off and the good finish has to go down and match whatever the surrounding area looks like.

If the floor finish has been destroyed over a large area, perhaps patchy over the whole floor space, the best method is to rent a huge buffer and do the whole floor with fine steel wool pads to lift the old finish and get down to raw wood. Sanding, with any grade sandpaper, is not recommended unless you have a good knowledge of the tools and materials. If you have never done it, it is very difficult to do without messing up the floor.

But the steel wool pads do not chew down the way sandpaper does, and you'll find that once over will remove most of the finish. If you are doing corners where the buffer will not reach, do it by hand. You will find it much easier if you use a short piece of

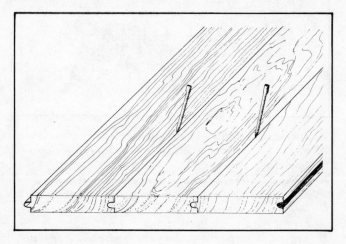

For squeaking floors or lifting boards nail finishing nails between the seams, setting them ⅛ inch and filling the tops with appropriately colored filler stick.

Machines are preferred for floor refinishing, and can often be rented. A large drum-type sanding machine with vacuum attachment is best for the main floor area, while a power edger does sides as shown above.

Hand scraping is sometimes needed at edges and in corners even when using an edger-sander. Be careful not to gouge, and go over enough times to create a good surface, sanding with the grain.

two-by-four covered with steel wool. The block allows you to press down and get more pressure. With all the finish off it is a simple matter to refinish, using oils or gym-seal or any of several good floor finishing materials on the market. Just follow the instructions on the can for the floor color desired. The main thing is to be sure the old finish is thoroughly wooled off, completely gone, or the new one will not take evenly and will look spotty.

If the area to be repaired is small, just a spot here or there, it is more difficult to make a close match but not impossible. First, conservatively apply floor finish remover and allow everything to dry out well after each application. For small patches of discolo-

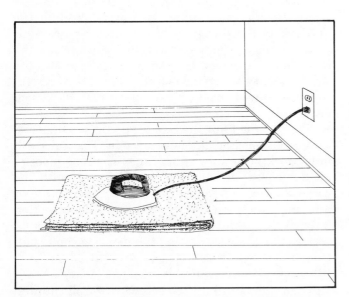

Use a slightly damp towel and hot iron to lift dents or prevent warping.

ration, where the floor is very dark, try a squirt or two of plain lighter fluid—it removes old finish and bleaches admirably for small areas.

For pet stains, try a mixture of Seven-Up and lighter fluid. Just apply with a rag, let set for a few minutes, wipe off, let completely dry, and reapply as necessary to totally lift the stain. Then refinish with oil, seal or wax as needed to match.

When spot refinishing hardwood floors be sure to "feather" the new finishing job into the surrounding old to make it fit in and match better. Work it out gently with a brush or rag to make it fit in.

Sugarpine (Softwood) Floors

Almost nonexistent in new homes, the old softwood floors were made largely of sugarpine, a clear softwood. They are beautiful, but terrible to maintain because they are so soft.

Repair methods are basically the same as with hardwood floors in all areas. You will find, however, that dents more readily "lift" out of the hardwood using a wet towel and iron than they do out of the softwood. Once the softer wood has been creased it does not bounce back so readily, if at all.

Some general thoughts to remember about softwood floors:
- If you are sanding, be extremely cautious; the wood is just like butter to a power sander.
- Floor finishes will take more of everything to do the same job as for hardwood; the softwood soaks it up like a sponge.

If you have a home with softwood floors, especially if you have children, the floors will be continuously dented without rugs to absorb some of the damage. Just dropping a metal toy makes a dent

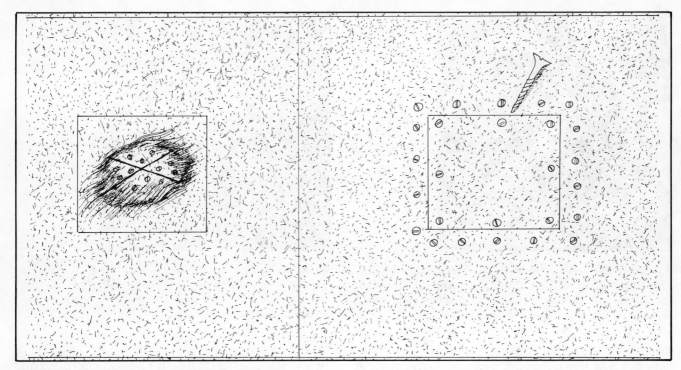

Cut the relief cuts carefully; in small damaged areas two will usually be enough. Then pull down with screws. For larger damaged areas, the damaged area must be removed and replaced with a new piece of particleboard

carefully fitted to match the hole. Wood screws are used to fasten the patch and edges of the existing floor to the subfloor.

that lasts forever, or until your next sanding. Rugs help protect the floors.

Softwood shrinks at a much faster rate and to a much greater degree than does hardwood. Seams will actually open up. For this reason, consider a "wet" finish that keeps the wood from drying out over a long period—as with a good floor oil or regular type motor oil (which also makes a good finish for hardwood floors). Just wipe the finish on, let soak, and wipe off the excess with an old towel.

Particleboard Underlayment

For economic reasons more and more homes are being finished with particleboard floors. Tiles, sheet, or carpet are then put over the board.

Generally speaking, not much can happen to particleboard. It is just there. The one thing, which does not happen often and yet can be devastating if it does, involves the house pipes. In colder regions of the country they can freeze, burst and soak a particleboard floor.

The particleboard expands at a rate that is alarming. A well-soaked floor can rise up beneath the flooring as high as six or eight inches. When it dries, the floor does not return to its previous condition.

In this case the only repair is to remove the floor covering and attack the board itself. After it has completely dried, use a rotary saw and a wide-cutting carbide blade and cut X patterns across the bubbles. These cuts provide relief and allow the underpart of the cuts to dry.

With everything dry, drill and pull the raised portions of the particleboard down with wood screws, countersinking the screws so the flooring cover will not hit them.

This pulling-down method will work for the smaller bubbles. If there are large swollen areas, the only repair is to cut out whole rectangles around the bubbles and throw them away and replace with appropriately cut new sections of board. Just set the blade on the rotary saw so that it only cuts the thickness of the particleboard and be very careful that the saw doesn't "kick" out of the cut as you lower it in.

When you cut out the repair spot in a whole rectangle, do not nail the new piece in. The nails will only work loose in a short time. The new piece of particleboard has to be screwed down, with the screws going down well into the plywood subfloor and on 8-inch centers. Use a good construction adhesive underneath the new piece, and also sink screws in the pieces *around* the new one you're putting in on 8-inch centers—to prevent edges from lifting on the old pieces.

When done, and all the screws are well countersunk, cover with a proper filler so that the repair job presents a smooth surface for flooring.

Carpet Repair

Replacing whole carpeted areas is not truly a repair and will not be covered here except to say that it is more complicated than it looks. Proper stretching and putting in the underfoam correctly can be tricky.

But elemental repairs are possible without going through the difficulties and expense of complete replacement.

For tears made by moving furniture or whatever, sewing may suffice. Just use correctly-colored heavy thread (sail thread) and a curved upholstery or sail needle and sew up the cut with close, tight stitches. Tie it well when done and the repair will probably outlast the rest of the carpet.

If sewing does not seem adequate, get a heat-tape strip the right length from the nearest carpet or flooring store—this is a piece of fabric covered with strips of meltable glue. Put the strip under the cut with gum side up, running the length of the slit, and cover it with a buffer cloth (old dishtowel) and iron the cut with the iron set on high. The iron melts the glue in a short time, mixing it with the fabric of the carpet and essentially welding the two together.

This same method can be used to fix whole sections of ruined or severely stained carpet. Cut out a square around the bad area, as small as possible. Then cut a new piece the exact size and weld it in with heat-tape strips all around the new piece. If you

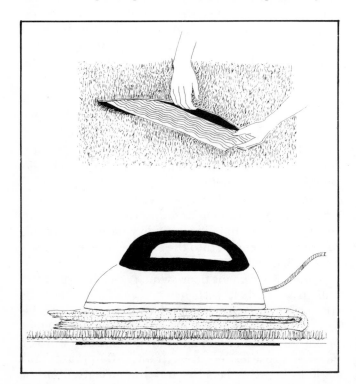

Put heat tape strip under the carpet tear, gum side up, running the length of the damage. Cover with a buffer cloth and iron the cut with a very hot iron.

both sew and tape, the repair is probably stronger than new carpet.

Stain removal is hard. There are so many different weaves and synthetic fabrics that using a bleach product can destroy the carpet. The best process for trying to remove stains is to use warm soap and water. If that does not work, use a strong detergent and if that does not work, learn to live with the spot. For those who have cats that have pulled up the little hooks of pile try putting a dab of quick dry epoxy in the pulled-up end and tucking it back down into the mesh backing, being sure to poke the end through the mesh. When the glue sets it will look and hold like new.

Linoleum

Linoleum isn't used much for floor covering today but the two things which most often go wrong with old linoleum floors are denting and tearing or cutting, mostly from moving appliances without lifting them.

In the case of dents, try a hot iron with a buffer towel. It does not always work, but sometimes it will do the job. There is no other effective way to lift dents.

For cuts, gently lift the edges of the cut and work glue carefully back under both sides. Then put wax paper down on the cut and weight it down with a book or something.

When the glue has dried, use an appropriate felt tip marker or markers to recolor the glue in the crack to match the surrounding color and/or pattern. Felt tip markers also can be used to recolor a place on the floor where a chair or appliance has scraped through the color.

Composition (Asphalt or Vinyl Tile) Flooring

Composition tile flooring, usually glued down on concrete or on particleboard, is easy to repair because it has been laid in individual squares and can be replaced with little effort.

To remove and replace a tile, which constitutes the basic repair for most tile floor problems, simply play a butane torch with a spreader head back and forth across the top of the tile from a height of five or six inches so the heat is evenly distributed and does not get hot enough to ignite the tile.

The edges will curl, and once the whole tile is warm it will lift out easily. Be sure to wear gloves. With the old tile out, scrape-clean the open space, apply a thin layer of tile adhesive, wait ten minutes and position the new tile carefully in place. It will seat and stick immediately, but if you find the edges are not flush with the surrounding tiles—play the torch around the sides to soften the tile just enough so it will lie down properly.

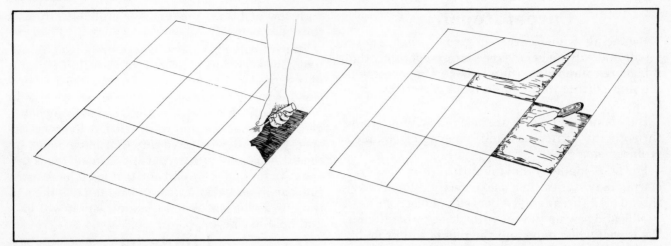

Broken tiles will come out easily when pried with a screwdriver. Lay a new bed of adhesive with a putty knife or other edge, and after waiting ten or fifteen minutes lay the new tile in.

The only tile problem that does not require replacement is when the tiles curl up or lift at the corners. This is usually due to age. Repair is simple, but might involve considerable time if there are many tiles pulling up. Use the butane torch and spreader head again, and after putting a small amount of glue under each corner and allowing the glue to set for ten minutes, soften the corners down into the glue by playing the torch back and forth from a distance of five to six inches. Do not let the torch come too close, as the tiles will easily melt and burn; it is better too slow than too fast.

Ceramic Tile Flooring

Becoming more popular as wood becomes more expensive, ceramic tiles create a durable and beautiful floor. Indeed, they have only two faults: (1) they sometimes crack, if they aren't set in right, and (2) they occasionally lift out of their grout.

Broken tile requires complete replacement, which is more difficult than dealing with composition tiles. The broken tile has to be "popped" out with a screwdriver, and then the opening has to be well brushed and cleaned. When you are certain the space is dry and clean, "fit" the new tile in place in the old grout. Do this dry, to make sure it is going to fit, and if there are any high spots where the grout pushes the new tile up or will not allow it to seat properly, carve these areas down using either a shop knife or coarse sandpaper. Make a close-fitting bed for the new tile or it will break like the old.

When the seat is just right and the tile does not wobble but sits firm, take it out and put down a 1/16-inch coating of construction adhesive. Set the tile in this immediately, press it firmly in place, and do not test it for two or three days.

For tiles which have lifted out of their grout but are still unharmed, the procedure is a simpler one. Just remove the tile, clean the blank space well—especially of dust, which has a way of filtering beneath the tiles when they are loose—and apply a 1/16-inch layer of construction adhesive which is applied like caulking, with a caulking gun. Then settle the tile in place immediately, pressing down firmly.

Again, cleanliness is the most important item when working with ceramic tile. Be certain the hole is clean and dust free, and then turn the tile over and clean the bottom with a damp rag, allowing it to dry well before putting it down. It is virtually impossible to glue the cracked tiles together, with any kind of glue, and then reset them on the floor. Such an application may work with countertops, but the load on the floor is too great and the tiles almost invariably recrack.

Concrete Floors

Since most concrete floors are covered with another kind of flooring, and since they are virtually indestructible anyway, there is very little to be said about repairing them.

They do crack, however, with curing and age. This is no big problem and the cracks are normally little more than hairlines. If you wipe a dry mixture of premixed cement into the exposed crack and let it cure, it will fix things up for years.

Sometimes cement floors which are left unpainted will give off dust with heavy use. This is simply from the abrasive nature of walking, and can be easily fixed by applying any of several good sealers or paints found at a local paint store. But a word of caution: those sealers are extremely flammable and toxic to breathe; be sure that you pay attention to the safety rules on the can. Many houses have been lost to careless use of sealers and flammable adhesives. The fumes are like gunpowder, especially when confined in a basement without proper ventilation.

Stone or Slate

Once limited to the patio, stone or cobble brick is fast becoming a decorator's floor for indoors as well as out.

Stone or brick flooring is virtually repair-free once in place, assuming it has been installed correctly, but there are two ailments which deserve mention.

Cobble brick floors have a tendency to become loose. Bricks start to wobble here and there when stepped on. This happens not because of improper seating, as might be expected, but because the buffer *between* the bricks has become compressed and allows them to move. For repair, mix a totally dry mixture of premixed masonry cement with pigment added to match the floor. Sprinkle this dry mixture around the loose bricks—still dry—and sweep and rub it down into the crack until it is packed in well and the brick no longer wiggles. Then use a flower sprayer or similar atomizer to put a fine mist of water around the crack and allow it to cure for two or three days, until it is well set. The floor will stay tight for years, and even then you only have to reapply the repair material should the brick become loose again.

Stone or flagstone flooring has a habit of cracking, especially the larger stones. There is no repair, as such, for cracked flagstones. You have to live with the crack. Once they break they also become loose and wobbly, and for this there is a repair. When the stone has become loose enough to pull out, take it straight up and out, being careful not to damage the grout around the stone. Then use construction adhesive (the same kind used for ceramic tile repair) and lay a ⅛-inch bed of glue in the empty space. Even this out with a straight stick or something else you can throw away, so the glue is a good, solid all-over bed for the wobbly or broken flagstone. Put the stone back in immediately, still being extremely cautious not to disturb the grout, and press it firmly but evenly into the glue. Put no further weight on the stone for at least two days, so the adhesive has time to cure.

For broken out or cracked pieces of slate or stone flooring, relay the stone piece which has broken out in a ⅛-inch glue base of construction cement. Let dry for several days before walking on it.

Discolored slate or stone floors can be recolored with appropriately colored drawing ink—the kind that does not wash out. There are literally hundreds of colors to use for matching. Check your local art store. Commercial stone quarry distributors also sell cleaning solutions that remove most stains.

When the color is good, a treatment of a whole stone or slate floor with lemon oil will give a low gloss that looks rich and holds for days.

Interior Walls and Ceilings

Essentially, interior walls and ceilings can be broken down into two categories: either lath and plaster or drywall. The repair methods are somewhat different for the two forms. Problems covered are those considered most common or most likely to occur, and the repair method suggested for each is the easiest and least expensive.

Lath and Plaster

Virtually no new homes are made of lath and plaster although it makes a strong wall and is viewed by many as more attractive than drywall. But it costs so much in labor to put in, and lath and plaster craftsmen are becoming so rare, that people can't afford it.

Many older homes have it and repairing it properly can be a significant part of owning an old home. Some of the more typical problems with lath and plaster are listed below.

Small holes, dents or chips are the most common plaster problems. Usually caused by pulling out nails that held pictures, or moving furniture, the plaster tends to mar in a little crater and the smallest nail can make a pockmark an inch across. The repair is basic, quick and simple. Get a gallon can of premixed drywall mud and use a putty knife or small drywall knife to fill the hole. Buy only the kind of drywall mud that *does not* have asbestos. Asbestos fibers, which they had in the old kind of mud, have been linked to certain forms of lung cancer, and it is dangerous to sand it without wearing a professional respirator mask. Just one quick application, a single swipe, and let dry for a day before sanding with fine sandpaper and painting to match. Take a paint sample from right next to the repaired spot; if you take a sample from across the room it might not match.

Holes of considerable size can be patched in lath and plaster this same way.

When the damaged spots get big, two inches or more across, the work becomes more involved. The mud must be put on in two steps, the first a thick coat to fill the hole, and then a thin coat once the first coat has dried completely, as a finish. The undercoat will crack when it dries, but the second coat will fill the cracks. On very large patches—a foot across or more—it may take three coats, the final coat being very thin and sloppy. You can thin the drywall mud with plain water. Sand after the final coat, with fine paper, taking off the lumps or buildup, and paint to match the surrounding area. Be sure to "feather" the patch into the old plaster and sand it to further fit it.

There is no way to save plaster which has started to separate from the lath, common in a ceiling after a bad leak. If it has already come loose, accept the loss and pull out what has come loose and is falling away and patch with drywall mud. This does not mean that you should jump to conclusions when you see a damp spot after a rain. First find and fix the leak, then let the plaster dry out completely, and it is probable that all you will have is a stain to paint over. Wet plaster often dries out safe and sound. But if it gets really soaked it will visually separate from the lath, or it might even drop on your rug, and then repair is necessary.

On large patches, be sure to work the first coat of drywall mud well into any and all exposed lath, so that it "catches" well and holds. This is especially vital on ceiling repair, for obvious reasons. Also, on large patches, use a *wide* drywall knife, six inches or better. It is almost impossible to get a smooth patch over a large area with a small knife. Sanding will take care of most mistakes. If it looks bad when you finish using the knife, don't worry; even the bumpiest ridges can be taken down with some sanding.

Hairline cracks are the most common problem with lath and plaster, but are also easy to fix. Scrape the crack with a paint scraper, down the long way, and not too heavy. The idea is to remove some of the paint and loose plaster to get a good bond with the patch. Then use a narrow drywall knife to run a thin layer of mud down the length of the crack, forcing it into the crack with steady pressure. Wipe off excess and allow to dry thoroughly overnight. Then sand with a light touch and paint to match. The crack will disappear.

Most plastered walls and ceilings are smooth, and repairs should match. But now and then the homeowner will run across a textured wall or ceiling, and a smooth repair will not be appropriate. The way to get a texture to match the old is to mix up a small amount of drywall mud into a gloppy sort of thick paint; just keep adding water until the consistency reaches thin fudge. Then wet a towel, or a mop, or a piece of scrap carpet, and pat some of the mixture onto the patch. Try different items until you find

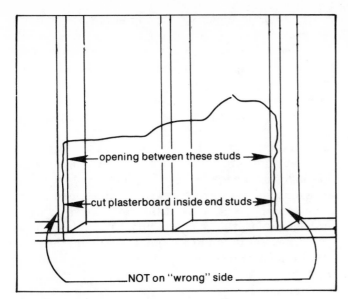

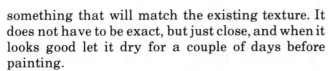

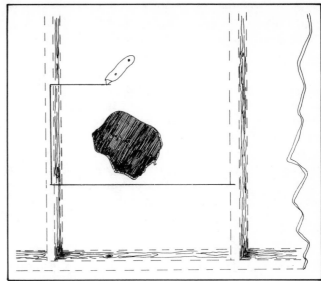

Cut out the damaged drywall with shopknife, nail and tape in the new. Don't worry that it doesn't look good right away; sanding will eliminate all rough appearances.

something that will match the existing texture. It does not have to be exact, but just close, and when it looks good let it dry for a couple of days before painting.

Drywall Walls and Ceilings

In most respects, repairing drywall is the same as repairing lath and plaster, except that it is easier.

Small holes, dents, and gouges from moving furniture or children playing can be fixed with a dab of premixed drywall mud. They also make a powdered form of drywall cement: spackling paste, joint cement, joint compound, joint mud, taping mud, sheetrock mud, rock mud, wallboard mud; it's all the same. This powdered mud will do a nice job, but it is hard to mix; so care must be taken to get the right texture for patching without lumps. Premixed varieties are available that come with proper patching consistency and the can can be resealed for future use. As with lath and plaster, just give the small hole, crack, dent or gouge a quick swipe with the mud on a small knife, let dry, sand, and paint to match.

You must paint drywall mud, by the way, even if it matches the white of the rest of your wall when dry. If you do not paint it the material will never adhere properly and a little will rub off every time you touch it. But as with plaster repair, be certain the patch is totally dry before applying paint. Wait overnight or longer.

Larger holes in drywall can be fixed in several ways, all simple. The easiest is to cut a square or rectangle around the hole, as small as possible. Then cut a piece of drywall (with a shop knife or saber saw) to fit snugly in the hole. Clean the edges of the hole and the cut patch of dirt and dust and apply wet drywall mud on the sides of the opening

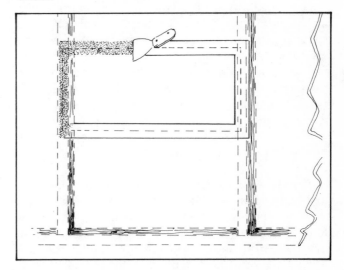

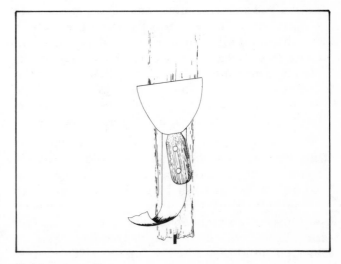

Taping drywall.

and around the patch and gently put the patch in place using the drywall mud as glue to hold it in. With extreme care, wipe off the excess mud and allow to dry completely.

When totally dry, sand the drywall lightly and "tape" all the seams. Taping drywall is tricky but easy to learn. You first apply a thin coat of drywall mud to the seam, about 3 inches wide, and put a precut piece of drywall paper tape on the seam. Do this for all four sides and again let dry for a few hours. When reasonably dry, apply another layer of mud over the tape—still thin, still about 3 inches wide, and feather this out into the surrounding wall. Let it dry well, sand lightly and paint to match the wall.

For truly large holes in drywall, cut the drywall out between studs or rafters, going from the middle of one stud to the next (the stud or rafter will be easy to find in a hole so big) and cut a new piece to fill the hole. Nail this new piece in place using drywall nails on 4-inch centers, so the repair section spans the whole distance between studs or rafters.

Tape the joint, taking your time and using a wide knife, sanding evenly between coats of mud if necessary to get a good looking seam. When it is done, and dry, paint to match.

Two points to remember about working with drywall mud, especially overhead. It stings in your eyes, so you might want to wear goggles or safety glasses when you work. And when you sand drywall mud it gives off a fine, irritating sneezy dust. If you have bronchial problems, use a nose-and-mouth cover.

Finally, we look at the most common and needless drywall repair job, which is sadly becoming more and more common: the lifting seam, or tape coming loose on a fairly new home. The problem is that the drywaller did not get enough mud under the tape during the original taping and the adhesive qualities did not take—another way of saying shoddy workmanship. The repair involves taking a six-inch wide drywall knife and putting new drywall mud in the seam. Just spread a layer of mud right over the lifted tape and paint, old wall and all. When it is dry, sand a bit and add another layer if necessary to "feather" it out into the wall for an even surface. When that is dry and sanded, paint to match.

For textures, as with lath and plaster, mix up a thick drywall mud, so it is like paint, and start experimenting with different objects to get a matching texture. Try sponges, sacking, or whatever it takes to look right. Most drywallers like to texture with a very heavy-nap paint roller, because it covers fast and thick. If the texture on your wall looks very even, you might try a heavy-nap roller. It will probably match perfectly.

On major problems such as burst pipes in ceilings or wind damage, do not try to save the drywall. Even with skyrocketing prices on building materials it is cheaper to buy new drywall. Just rip out the whole damaged sheet, pull the nails and apply a new sheet, and tape to fit in.

Don't underestimate the dirtiness of working with drywall. Most work with sheets of drywall is done with a sharp shopknife; just cut and break on the line. But now and then it is necessary to cut with a handsaw or saber saw (to cut a piece out of the wall), or with a hand drywall saw which looks like a keyhole saw. No matter what the saw, the sawdust is unbelievable. It goes everywhere and gets into everything. But if you have someone hold up the open end of a running vacuum cleaner hose right along the cut you are making, most of the dust can be eliminated.

Other Wall Coverings

Wood Paneling can be patched with appropriately colored wood filler compound. If you have a lot of paneling it wouldn't hurt to keep a couple of tubes on hand. They are inexpensive and easy to store. Check the color by application and store in a cool dry place. The filler really works well for nail holes when you pull out a picture, or to fill in dents or tears. As far as the general finish goes, there are many good finishing agents for wood paneling. They all leave a shine and furnish adequate protection, but are generally expensive. For the money it is hard to beat plain old-fashioned wood or lemon oil—which does not cost as much as the spray cans and helps preserve the wood better.

Barn wood is the classic example of raw wood walls. It can be repaired by replacement, just as with external siding. Be careful when hammering, as the wood is soft and interior hammer dents show when light changes angles. If you do make a dent, it can be lifted out with a damp towel and hot iron which works well for most dented wood problems. If pieces of the wood wall have been broken out, do not jump to an expensive replacement conclusion. Before tearing the rest of the board out, consider gluing the piece back in. Use a strong, clear-drying glue and follow directions on the tube carefully. Do not rush anything. If a whole long piece of wood has split off, it would not hurt to "peg" the repaired section. After the glue has set and dried thoroughly, drill a couple of small holes up through the split piece into the larger one (just use a drill bit the size of wooden matches); then push some wooden matches with ends soaked in glue up into the hole. When the glue is dry, cut them off with a razor blade or utility knife. Stain the little ends of the matches by dabbing a bit of color on them: felt tip pen, wood stain or

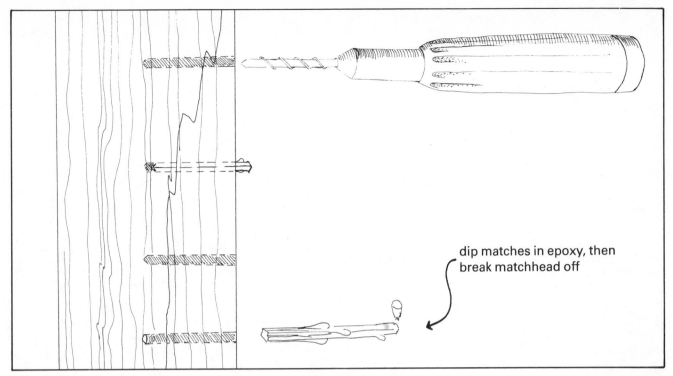

dip matches in epoxy, then
break matchhead off

After repairing wood by gluing the old piece back in place, add extra strength with "pegging." All you need *are some matches, a screwdriver, some epoxy, a color marker, and a utility knife or razor blade.*

whatever you have to match the color. This pegging is not truly necessary, but gives the repair extra strength and will help if the siding is low enough to get bumped by furniture.

Wallpaper Repair Wallpaper dropped out of vogue for a while but is becoming popular again as a covering. It is a virtually repairless surface. If it goes bad, start from scratch because it is usually patterned and hard to match. One common problem is "lifting," when the paper comes up or bubbles. If it lifts on a seam, simply apply a dab of wallpaper wheat paste and press it back down. If the bubble is in the middle of a sheet, slice with a razor blade, use a toothpick to gently work paste back under into the bubble and then press down. Do not use mucilage glue or airplane cement. Flour and water paste or commercial wheat paste can be taken off the surface with a damp rag once the repair is finished.

Many people pay a contractor or handyman to strip off or put up wallpaper, but this is one job that offers savings to the homeowner without potential hazard or unprofessional-looking results.

Remove old wallpaper unless it adheres firmly to the surface, especially where the seams join and at the edges in the ceiling or at any protruding surface such as a windowsill or molding. You can tell whether or not the covering adheres firmly by cutting out two square feet of the wallpaper you plan to use and applying paste to half of it. Apply the whole square, which means that one half will hang loose, and let stand overnight. Then tear off the unpasted section, which will pull up pasted paper as well. If the old wallpaper beneath the newly pasted part comes off too, then you know the old wallpaper has to be removed.

If there is a plastic coating on the old wallpaper, use an alkyd primer-sealer before applying the new wallpaper. Use a similar coating over old wallpapers that have become dry and chalky.

Depending upon the tenacity of the old wallpaper, you may have to try several methods of removal. The first and easiest approach is to saturate the wallpaper with hot water and then scrape it off. If this does not work, try a commercial wallpaper remover to heighten water penetration and speed the job, or rent a wallpaper steamer for large scale removal. Never use a steamer near fine furniture, cabinets, or floors. Experienced contractors prefer to use them only in empty rooms, with windows open.

If you are removing foil covering or one overcoated with water-resistant material, use sandpaper or an abrasive of some type to bite shallowly into the surface. This will enable you to reach the water-absorbent material. Then saturate, using a light mist from a hand sprayer or sponge.

Once the wallpaper has been removed, be sure to work off all adhesive; hot water applied with a slightly abrasive pad will usually do it. Be careful

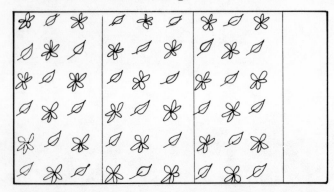

1—In a drop-match pattern, once you line up the marks, you will find the first strip has the full pattern at the top. The number two strip will have a half-pattern at the top; the number three strip will also have the full pattern at the top. These three strips illustrate a drop match pattern. Note that every other strip is the same at the top.

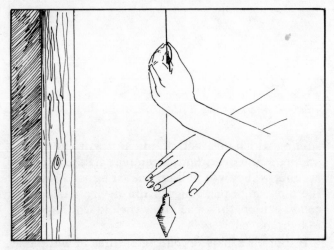

2—One strip (less ½ inch) to the right of the door, fasten plumb line from ceiling. Chalk the string and, holding near the bottom, snap a line onto the wall. Measure ceiling height. Allow 3 inches extra top, 3 inches at bottom.

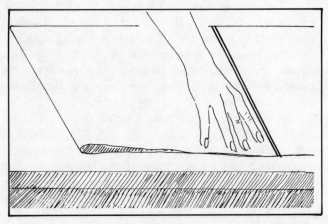

3—After pasting smoothly, fold to paste so edge ends up just short of center of strip, pattern up. Fold other edge to just beyond the edge of other fold, which should have a few inches without adhesive. Do not crease folds.

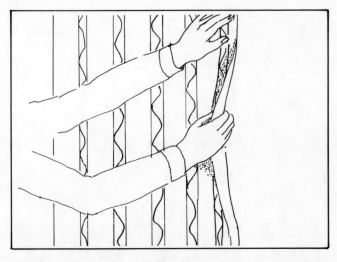

4—Unfold top part of strip only. Position near ceiling, leaving 3 inches to trim later. Line up the right of the strip with the plumb line.

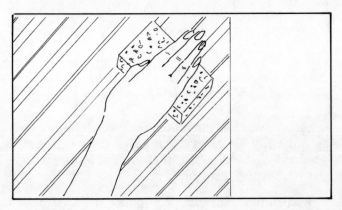

5—Smooth strip, working from center to edges. Unfold bottom, align with plumb line, smooth out entrapped bubbles with sponge. Small bubbles disappear with drying.

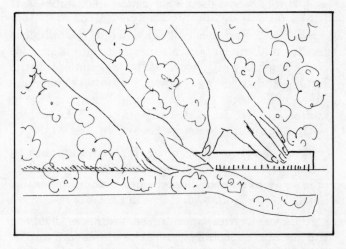

6—Use ruler with knife or razor blade to trim top, bottom and around door frame. Wipe off paste with wet sponge. Smooth entire strip. Roll down edges with a seam roller. Don't use roller on flocked wall coverings. Tap seams with sponge to avoid matting flock pile.

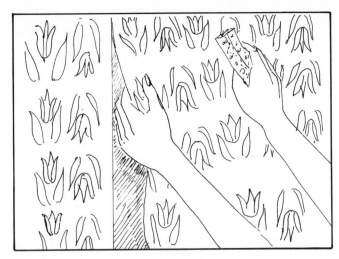

7—*Hang succeeding strips. Carefully match pattern at left edge of new strip with previous strip. Butt edges, sponge and roll edges.*

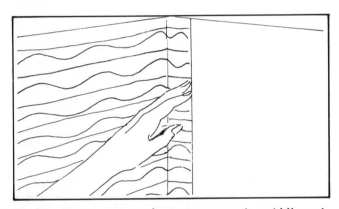

8—*At corner: measure edge-to-corner at tip, middle and baseboard. Take widest measure; add ½ inch. Measure next strip. Add ½ inch. Drop plumb this distance from corner. Follow plumb; apply, match pattern and lap a corner.*

9—*Windows: measure ceiling to frame. Add 1 inch. Cut vertical strip, apply so it extends over top of frame 1 inch. Trim around frame. Match pattern; use short lengths above, below frame.*

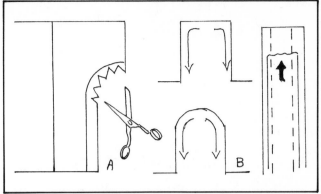

10—*Application at arches: (a) to prevent fraying at edges make small cuts ½ inch apart so wallpaper will wrap on the inside of the arch without wrinkling; (b) if doing the top section of the arch, cut your strip so it is long enough to start hanging from the inside in the middle, then continue down each side. The mismatch will not be seen underneath. Remember to (c) leave ½ inch overlap on each edge of the wallpaper used underneath, ¼ inch of which goes under the covering used on the outside. Leave ¼ inch space between edge of arch and wallpaper covering placed as an overlap, to prevent fraying or peeling at overlapping edge.*

not to gouge the walls. Spackle to smooth out any depressions. Also tape and spackle joints between preformed wall components such as plywood or drywall, because joints are often improperly joined. Once the spackle has dried, use a primer-sealer so the porous components won't suck in the adhesive which will make future wallpaper removal very difficult.

If walls are old and appear porous, or you have old wallpaper with a fine dust or powder you can't remove completely, treat the area with a glue size or emulsion bonding agent. There are several types on the market: cold water natural powder and the jellized size risk mildew under materials that do not breathe, such as vinyl, foil, or Mylar. For these products use a synthetic size.

Another possible answer to minor irregularities in surface and adhesive control, particularly for sensitive materials such as silk and textiles, is paper lining. The acid-free type is more expensive but avoids possible chemical damage. Be sure to leave ⅛-inch gap at ceiling, baseboard, window, and door casings so the wallpaper can bond to the wall; this will prevent lifting.

With the wall properly prepared, you are ready to begin hanging. Roll wallpaper out on a paste table. Trim off selvages using carefully placed straightedge. Locate the point at which you want the pattern to begin on the wall; this is where the paper will meet the ceiling edge. You will be looking for the point at which a full pattern begins. Be sure the top of the material is to your left. From the point selected, measure the height of the wall, and add 2 to 3 inches extra from the top point of the pattern, and the same at the bottom. Use a straightedge at right angles and cut the strip off with a razor blade.

If the wallpaper has a drop-match pattern you will have to move down to catch a full pattern, which leaves a great deal more than 3 inches of excess. Cut off all but 3 inches at top and bottom to prevent extra wallpaper from interfering with hanging.

With a quarter-drop pattern (even more complicated than a drop-match) use four rolls; number each roll, one through four, for each step in the pattern. After marking numbers, match join-points so the second, third, and fourth strips in a sequence move along the pattern as you go to the succeeding strips. If stiffness makes it difficult to trim selvages, leave them on the first and second strips and match up the pattern while hanging them. This means one selvage goes beneath the other, and top selvage flaps over the edge of the pasted-down wallpaper. Then cut through both selvages to end up with a double-cut seam. Lift up the wallpaper that covers the cut-off selvage which ended up underneath; remove strip of cut selvage; readhere edge of strip. Repeat for remaining strips.

Lay strips face down on a table, making sure you have a smooth surface. Again, place the top of the wallpaper to your left. Load a 7-inch paint roller with a ⅜-inch nap with just enough paste so it doesn't drip. Draw it down the middle of the strip, starting about 2 or 3 inches from the top end so you can leave unpasted the area to be trimmed off. Continue halfway down the strip. Work the paste on this strip toward both edges. This gives a smooth coat and avoids smears. The roller also contributes to a more even coat. Repeat procedure for the bottom half of the strip.

The accompanying illustrations offer basic steps in matching, cutting, and hanging.

Tile Tile walls are commonly used in bathrooms but are becoming prevalent in kitchens as well. They have two problems: either the adhesive comes loose or the tiles crack. If the adhesive is the culprit, simply buy some tile adhesive and reglue the loose piece. Directions for the process are on the glue can. If one is loose, however, it is possible that there are others and you should check this by using your fingers to gently "rock" each tile. If the glue is coming loose the tile will move, and it is easy to pull the tiles out for replacement. For cracked tiles the obvious solution is to pull out the broken tile and glue a new one in. Sometimes a replacement tile is not available or cannot be found, and it becomes necessary to reuse the old tile. Take out the cracked pieces and glue them together with a *good* glue. Quick drying epoxy-base glue is best for this application. Let the glue dry well, for a full day, so that it is properly hard, then reglue the tile in place on the wall with a thick base of tile adhesive to give it a cushion and prevent recracking.

Several companies have recently made available vinyl plastic wall panels. Gouges or dents will not iron out, however, and must be filled with appropriately colored filler; a wood filler will work. The finishes will "melt" if hit with something hot and there is no repair except replacement of the whole sheet if a filler doesn't work. You cannot remelt the finish and reform it. If, however, you cannot get a new piece of vinyl sheeting, you might try cutting the melted piece out and refilling with fiberglass putty. When it is hard and well set, paint to match with plastic model cement, either gloss or matt as the situation dictates.

The final type of plastic described here is not typically a wall covering, but might be. Countertops are covered with this hard-surfaced sheathing, and it sometimes runs up the wall. Generally the only problem is that the glue allows it to come away from the undersurface. If this occurs, reglue it with cement from the local lumberyard. Chips, which can happen, virtually cannot be fixed and must be lived with. Some of these surfaces will get a wrinkle or dimple if something hot comes in contact with it. Heat an iron and hold it a half inch or so over the dimpled area to repair. Too close and you will burn it, too far and the fix won't take. As the heat softens the surface it will go back to its previous shape and texture. Remove the iron, and allow the surface to cool slowly at room temperature.

Windows, Screens, and Drapes

There was a time when properly repairing windows was one of the things few people could do easily. Homeowners had to mix their own putty, which is tricky at best and disastrous at the worst, and cut their own glass. Most people gave up and just called the glazer. For the uninitiated, just cutting a pane of glass the right size is almost impossible.

But things have changed drastically. Premixed, plastic glazing compound comes in small, inexpensive cans. You can get precut glass panes at little extra cost from paint and glass stores and even some hardware stores.

The main thing to remember is to wear gloves, avoid cutting, and take your time.

Windows

Standard Panes, Wooden Window The classic paned window, which has been around for centuries, is probably the easiest to repair.

If possible, replacement glass for broken window panes should be tempered to prevent future breakage. This safety precaution is particularly important for sliding doorwalls and for storm windows.

When you have a broken pane of glass, the first step is to break out the rest of the broken glass. Push it out with a stick and steady gentle pressure. Wear gloves. When all the glass has been broken out, clean out all the remaining old putty and use a dull knife or chisel to scrape out the wooden channel where the glass fits. It is called a rabbet.

With the rabbet now clean, measure the size of the replacement window needed and take off just a bit, maybe a sixteenth of an inch. Have a piece of glass cut to the correct size and same thickness. Buy a small can of window glazing compound, a putty knife and some glazing points. For the do-it-yourselfer it is easier to use glazing points that are shaped like folded little arrows rather than the flat ones.

Position the glass in the rabbet and use the putty knife to jam the glazing points in place as per instructions on the glazing point box.

Two glazing points on each side of the glass should hold it securely.

Glazing, the actual putting in of the putty, tends to be easy if you relax and aren't too fussy.

First roll the putty between your hands to make a long tube about ⅜ inch thick. Press this tube gently into the corner of the window glass, where it meets the rabbet, so the tube goes all the way around the pane.

Then take the putty knife, and holding it at an

Push the glazing points straight with even pressure and don't push against the glass too hard.

After a bit of practice you'll find the excess putty just seems to roll down away from you.

angle use it to compress the putty down into the joint.

Do not "cut" the putty or shave it off, but mash it as you pull the knife along the tube of putty. The excess putty will ooze out the sides; the part that gets mashed down should form a nicely beveled edge.

Unless otherwise specified on the can, do not paint until the glazing compound has had a few days to set in and cure.

Large Wooden Windows with Nailed Stops Many homes built in recent years have simple wooden windows with large sections of glass held in by nailed strips of wood known as stops instead of glazing points and putty.

Repair is easy. First remove all the broken glass, wearing gloves and safety goggles because glass flies all over when it snaps and little, undetectable pieces can damage your eye. Clean out all the glass.

With all the glass gone it is time to remove the outside stops, the wooden "lips" that hold the window in place.

This can be done one of two ways. You may carefully take a wide wood chisel and work the stop loose by prying, but excessive care must be taken to avoid denting the wood. Or you can use a very thin, long nail punch to drive the finishing nails through the other side of the stop.

Either method demands great care and patience. Number or identify the stops and make certain they go back in *exactly* the order they came out. Houses settle with age and window frames may move a bit. If you do not put them back the way they came out they probably will not fit.

With the stops removed use a chisel to clean the dried caulking out of the place where the window will set. Then measure the opening and get a piece of glass cut to fit, but again slightly smaller to avoid problems.

While you are at the hardware or glass store get a small caulking gun and a tube of window caulking compound. It won't hurt to have the gun around for other uses, and it is not overly expensive.

At the glass store tell the clerk the type of window you are putting in and ask what size glass you should be using and whether or not it has to be crystal or plate. With free expert advice available you might as well use it.

Lay a bead of caulking around the entire window opening, all the way into the corner where the stop meets the sill. Allow to set a few minutes, so it will not be runny and sticky, and then put the window in place. Wear gloves and work it back into position slowly, a little at a time, all around the glass. Window glass will bend a little, especially larger plates, but the instant it warps too much it shatters. Go a little at a time, all around. Work it back into the caulking until it is well stuck and then put the stops in.

Insert the top one first, nailing with 6d galvanized finishing nails. Nail with all caution. A piece of cardboard or fiberboard against the glass will help protect it from the hammer.

Follow the edge of the glass with the stops and do not cause undue strain by pushing the stops back in too hard against the glass. The whole window frame might be slightly askew, and you can't fix it by "bending" the glass.

Wooden Window with Routed Sash Rails and Stiles Some windows have the glass installed at the factory, with in carved out and routed grooves. When such windows break repair is very difficult.

It is necessary to literally hack out the glass from the front of the rails and stiles with a chisel or knife, pick the glass out, sand all the rails and stiles so they look good (and they almost never will), individually cut the new panes to fit this ragged hole, and putty the glass in.

These windows are very expensive. They should be free.

Many new homes have aluminum window systems for economic reasons and ease of installation. They are also the easiest to repair if they have been installed correctly. Repair is simply a matter of removing the broken glass, taking out the screws that hold the frame together and putting in the appropriately cut repair piece of glass.

You will find a plastic piece of permanent insulation barrier that serves as a caulking strip. Make sure this goes around the new glass just as it went around the old piece. Then screw the frame back together.

The builder may have installed the frame wrong by nailing down those portions of the frame which are supposed to be loose and unscrewable. If this is the case, the nails must be carefully worked up and out with a screwdriver or catspaw before you can effect a regular repair.

Replacing Wooden Windows with Aluminum The main thing about replacing wood windows with aluminum is not to take too much out. Remove all the weatherstrips with a screwdriver; take out the old wooden window; clean the opening—but leave the sill and stops in place. Now the window is preframed and you simply buy aluminum windows which will nail into the framed opening. Aluminum windows are available in a wide variety of sizes.

Remember to caulk under the edges with colored caulking when nailing in the new window.

Installing Prefabricated Wooden Windows in Old Openings Again, remove only what is necessary to get the opening down to the size of the new window assembly. Never remove any structural frame members. Take out the old weatherstrips and windows, then clean the sills and sides and fit the new window into the opening, nailing in with 10d finishing nails. Fill holes, and paint.

Picture and/or Plate Windows Repair methods are the same for large windows as they are for small. The broken glass goes out, then you clean, caulk, and put the new glass in.

But for large picture windows or store plates there are some added cautions to make the job safer and easier.

Always wear gloves, and get somebody to help you when it is time to put the new window in. It is extremely difficult and dangerous to do it alone.

Watch warpage. Large pieces of glass are especially prone to twisting and breakage. Do not force anything, ever. It will all come apart on you. When you get the new piece of glass cut, give yourself a good ⅛ inch of play all around, plenty of room, and caulk liberally when you put the new piece in.

Finally, evaluate the kind of window you are putting in and how much money you want to spend.

Plate is very flat, and quite expensive, but virtually cancels out the "wobbly" effect common on many large windows. Crystal is much less expensive, and every bit as good for letting light in. However, it will have a wobble here and there, and if the picture window you are putting in or repairing is for unobstructed viewing, you might want to go to plate.

Installation or repair methods are the same for either one.

When and How to Replace a Faulty Window

Even if your home is considered old and you've repaired and repainted and refinished many parts of it, you probably haven't replaced the windows. If your windows are in poor condition, they can be weatherstripped and you can add storms, but also consider replacing the units altogether.

How can you tell when it's time to replace windows? Be on the lookout if your windows just don't seem to be doing what they're supposed to. Does the outside view seem blurry? Do you always have to prop your window open because it won't stay that way by itself? Do you constantly have to caulk and weatherstrip your windows because of the drafts? With enough "yes" answers to those questions, you may have reached the point of no return where your time and money on repairs simply aren't worth the investment.

Until a few years ago this was a very costly undertaking, but many window manufacturers today are offering custom-fit windows which require no structural alteration. By following the instructions here, you should be able to do the job efficiently and effectively.

1—Remove window trim to free sash.

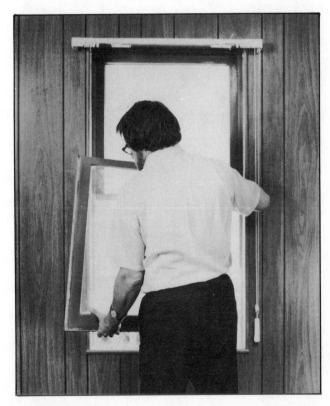

2—Then remove sash.

3—Using a screwdriver for leverage, remove wooden channels and all other obstructions.

5—When the unit is assembled, make sure that it fits squarely into the space. If space is not square use wooden shims to make window fit. Do not bend the frame to make it fit the space.

4—Assemble the new unit according to manufacturer's instructions. The next three photos show how one unit goes together.

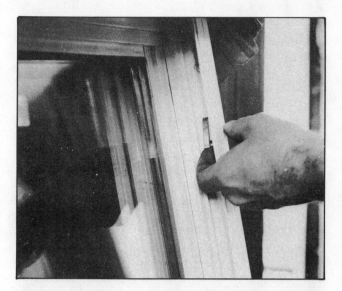

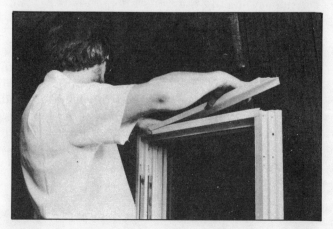

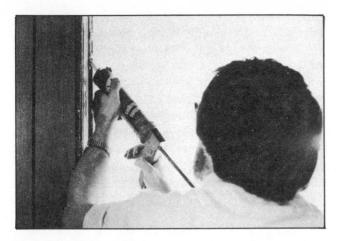

6—Remove the window and apply generous amount of caulking before installation.

7—Set window into the opening and tighten down the screw at one corner. Then square and plumb the unit for final adjustment.

8—Fasten the remaining sections of the window in place as shown in the next two photos. As you tighten down the screws, make sure you do not bend the unit to meet the wall. If wall is warped, use a shim behind the window to maintain square.

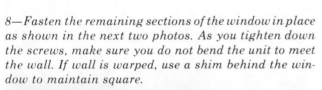

9—Install sashes according to the manufacturer's instructions.

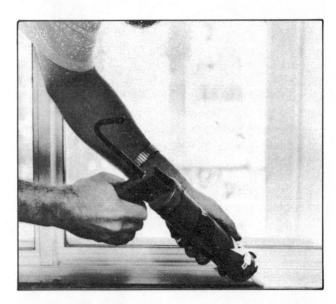

10—Caulk between the new window and the inside wall.

11—*Put up new molding unit around window. Photo courtesy of Season-all Industries, Inc.*

How to Weatherstrip Windows

To weatherstrip your windows and doors you'll need a hammer, nails, screwdriver, tin snips and tape measure. It usually takes less than one-half hour per window. You have a choice of installing at least three different types of weather stripping.

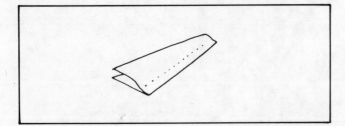

Metal Strip This strip is installed into the channel of the window or door so that it is virtually invisible. Because this weather stripping is metal, it is very durable. It doesn't need much maintenance but is somewhat difficult to install. It costs about $2 per window.

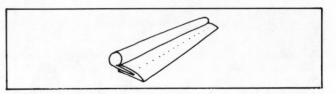

Rolled Vinyl It is available with or without metal backing, is durable, easy to install, but visible. It costs under $2 per window.

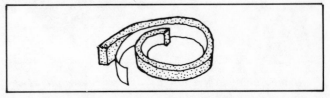

Foam Rubber with Adhesive Backing The least expensive, it is extremely easy to install but is also the least durable. It breaks down quickly, particularly where friction occurs, so you may be back weather stripping next autumn. Cost is pennies per foot.

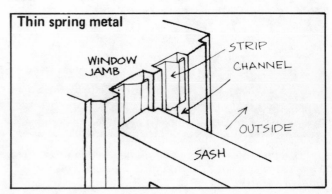

1—*Install by moving sash to the open position and sliding strip in between the sash and the channel. Tack in place into the casing. Do not cover the pulleys in the upper channels.*

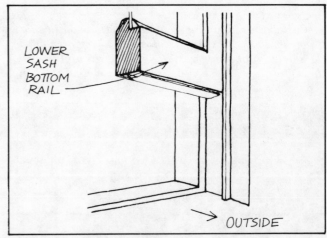

2—*Install the strips the full width of the sash on the bottom of the lower sash bottom rail and the top of the upper sash top rail.*

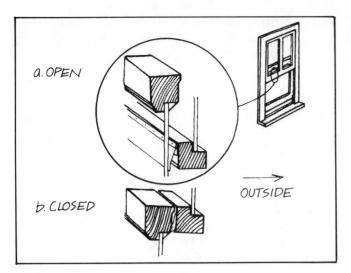

3—Then attach a strip the full width of the window to the upper sash bottom rail. Countersink the nails slightly so they won't catch on the lower sash top rail.

Leaded or Stained-Glass Windows Unless you are really committed to doing your own repair work it might be best to leave leaded or stained-glass windows to the experts. They are very tricky, and in the case of antique windows a great deal of beauty can be lost by making a small mistake.

Minor repairs can be done to the lead by using a soldering iron, just one of the little electric gun types, with resin core solder. Just apply the heat and solder simultaneously, and once the solder has filled the hole or dent, back off *instantly*.

If you are attempting to repair a broken out piece, carefully remove all the broken glass and reconstruct the broken piece on some cardboard. Make a template and take it to a glass cutter for a replacement piece. Also take some of the glass with you for a sample of the proper color.

Then use a pair of wire cutters or diagonal cutters to snip the leaded portion of the window as shown in the illustration.

Fold all these little pieces of lead up and out and put in the new piece of glass. Then fold them back down over the glass, ever so gently, and use the soldering gun to heat and fill the cracks and cuts made by the wire cutter.

It is really very difficult and not recommended for any except the totally committed or desperate.

Sticking Windows Although not strictly a repair, windows with wooden frames that stick and will not open are an irritation that deserves mention. Usually the reason is excessive painting and repainting of the windows so they are actually too big with the added layers of paint to move easily in the frame. In other cases the cause is humidity that makes the wood swell. For either situation the repair is the same.

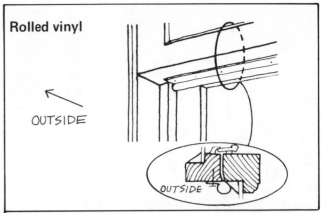

1—Nail on vinyl strips on double-hung windows as shown. A sliding window is much the same and can be treated as a double-hung window turned on its side.

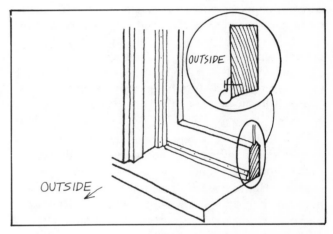

2—Tilting windows should be weatherstripped with the vinyl nailed to the window casing so that, as the window shuts, it compresses the roll.

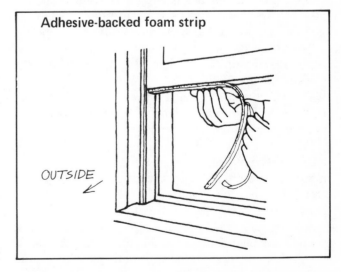

Install adhesive backed foam, on all types of windows, only where there is no friction. On double-hung windows, this is only on the bottom (as shown) and top rails. Other types of windows can use foam strips in many more places.

Pull the slider strips off—they are much like the stops on a permanent window—and pull out the whole window, with frame.

Use a non-filling rasp to take some wood off from the outside, about a sixteenth-inch off each side, and then put the window back, using the same holes for the nails.

Screens

Screen repair is not only an easy, inexpensive job that looks good when you are done, it can even be fun.

The type of repair depends on the type of screen. Most people use metal screening, but you will also find plastic, especially on sliding glass doors and other large applications. To be sure, plastic screening will not rust, which is a very big plus. Metal screens, especially in coastal areas, seem to rust out as fast as you get them in. But plastic screens have not been really perfected yet, and they seem to stretch with the heat of the sun and weather. It is almost impossible to keep plastic screens from looking slightly tired and baggy; particularly if you have children or pets that run into or lean on the screens.

In either case, the repair method is the same, but your choice of materials should be carefully studied before you begin the repair.

Wood Screens All around the outside edge and across the middle you will find small nailing strips of wood which hold the screen material on. Using a claw hammer or wide screwdriver, pry the strips off and remove all the nails. The nails will be rusty and you might as well throw them away and buy new ½-inch galvanized brads for replacement. But remember how the strips came off or number them, so you can put them back in *exactly* the same order.

Now lay your screen material on the frame and cut the screening so it just slightly overlaps the nailing strips.

Cut the screening with either a very good and tight set of tinsnips, or a very poor set of scissors you do not care about.

When the new piece is cut, put the nailing strips back on, stretching the screen material a little so it is tight. Do not pull it hard, just firmly, and nail the strips on six-inch centers. Do the top and bottom first, then the sides, then the middle.

As an aid to getting the screening in the right place some people use a staple gun, the kind used on insulation, and tack the screening in place all around before nailing down the strips.

Also, while you are repairing the screens it is a good time to check the tightness of the frames. Examine the corners for looseness. If there is a problem get some metal corner-brackets (the little L-shaped things) and screw them in place with short wood screws. A touch of glue in the corners will help hold until your regular maintenance program comes due.

Aluminum Frame Screening Not as strong as wood screens, aluminum screens really amount to a small metal frame with a kind of rubber strip that runs all around.

It is better to replace with plastic screening, because it is pliable enough to insert into the little groove and still allow the rubber strip to fit correctly into the slot.

Cut the screening big enough to overlap the groove ⅛ inch or so, and lay it across the frame in position. Then position the plastic strip over it and press it in all around, a bit at a time, gently pressing the strip in place with the fingers.

Do not worry if the frame feels loose and wobbly, even with the screen on tight. Aluminum screen frames are not particularly rigid and get their strength from the larger window frame once in place.

Do not stretch the screen as you put it on. The screen will be taken up by the tube and groove when you press it down, which will adequately stretch the material.

Screen Doors and Sliders Essentially, fixing screen doors is exactly the same as fixing windows, but more so. Wooden screen doors have nailing strips, the same as wooden windows, and metal sliding doors have the plastic strip and groove, as do aluminum windows. Just cut the material the right size and use the same method as you would use with a window.

If you have a wooden screen door without a wire with a turnbuckle to keep it tight, this might be a good time to put one in. Just buy a turnbuckle kit at the hardware store and put it in diagonally from top to bottom. Instructions come with the kit. Do not overtighten, but make it snug to keep the door from sagging.

If you have pets or children, you can install a plywood (¼ inch) screen on the bottom half of the door. Tack it to the screen nailing strips on the outside and it will keep your screen from getting torn out . . . for awhile. Nothing is impervious to children and pets forever.

Quick Fixes Often a cut in a screen will occur on the hottest night of the year, at the height of mosquito season or just when the hardware store will be closed all weekend. You might try "sewing" the damaged area to repair the cut quickly. Simply take some thin wire and patch the cut by working the wire back and forth through the screen to sew up the tear or cut.

If you do not have any wire, thread will do fine on a temporary basis.

Many discount and hardware stores are offering

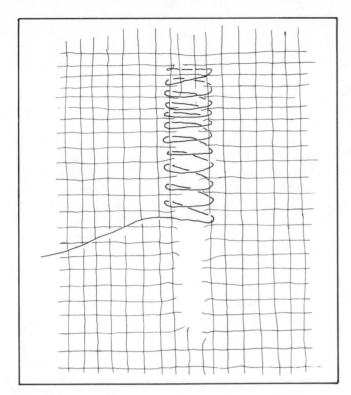

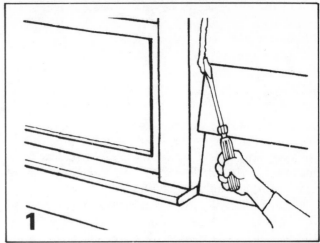

Before applying caulking compound, clean the area around the window of paint build-up, dirt, or deteriorated caulk with solvent and a putty knife or large screwdriver.

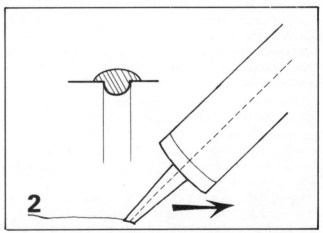

Drawing a good bead of caulk will take a little practice. First attempts may be a bit messy. Make sure the bead overlaps both sides for a tight seal.

screen repair kits and the like. They get the job done but often cost more money than it is worth. You should buy precut screening according to your window size and put it in. If you own a home, savings can be substantial by purchasing a whole roll of screening material and keeping it stored in the basement or storage area.

Drapery Ripout Repair

One of the more common problems with the recurring fashion demand for wide and heavy draperies is that they keep pulling out of the wall.

The repair is relatively simple. Whether drywall or lath and plaster, use the expanding wing nut—the kind with wings which open up when they get past the wall surface—or a "molly" to rehang the drapery rod. This will usually take care of the problem. If not, alongside each edge of the window (and it *has* to be there for structural purposes) you will find a stud. Use a 3-inch wood screw with thread all the way, and a round head with wide washers, to screw the drapery rod holder to the wall. It will not pull out again.

A wide bead may be necessary to make sure the caulk adheres to both sides.

Doors

Most people wait until their doors refuse to open or close before they worry about repair. Steps should be taken long before this stage is reached, however, because poorly functioning doors can cause a great deal of unnecessary frustrations.

A good maintenance program will catch most door problems before they become destructive, but if you are buying a new or old place or did not start your program in time to catch the problems, below are listed common door ailments and their cures.

Finishes

Weathered external doors are a common problem in older homes that have been neglected. Weathered-out doors are particularly sad because they are often those beautiful old paneled doors which you simply cannot replace.

Of course after a certain point, once the panels are completely cracked out, there is very little you can do except replace the door. But if the weathering is not too extensive and the cracking has not decimated the wood completely, there are some measures you can try.

First, take the door off and clean it as well as you can, working with a wire brush. Once it is clean, rub it with linseed oil, even if it had been painted; this will get into the cracks and help stabilize shrinkage.

Then work a filler into the door, all over—a good tight filler—and sand when dry. Do not be afraid to oversand because what you are working for is a smooth surface. Paint with a top-quality enamel, working in several thin coats rather than one thick one. Do not rehang the door until the paint is totally dry and cured which could be as long as two days. You want the wood to be well protected before subjecting the door to the elements.

Hinges

Rotted Out Exterior Hinges Another common problem with older homes occurs when weather rots out the hinges: rough weather and damaging elements work back up under the hinge plates and soak the wood until it rots.

Repair is difficult, but not impossible. First remove the door, and the hinges, and clean and pick everything out of the damaged areas under the hinge plates. Use a screwdriver to pick the rotten wood out—all of it.

With everything clean, mix up some epoxy glue—the kind that comes in two tubes—and dip the non-striking ends of matches into the glue and poke them down into the old screw holes; leave them in there, with plenty of glue on them. They will glue themselves in tightly, and you should jam as many into each hole as will fit, on both the door (if it is rotted out) and the frame. Just let them stick out for the moment; you can cut them off later when the glue is good and dry.

Now, wearing rubber gloves, "fill" all the torn out wood spots with epoxy, mashing it well in at first so it sticks, then leveling it off to meet the level of the wood. What you are doing, in effect, is rebuilding the wood with epoxy, reconstructing the rotted-out portions.

When the epoxy is well set—at least 24 hours—break off the matches and file or sand everything down so that it is even and smooth.

Then drill small pilot holes and screw the hinges back in place and rehang the door exactly as it was, taking care to tighten all screws snugly, but not with massive torque which could strip them out.

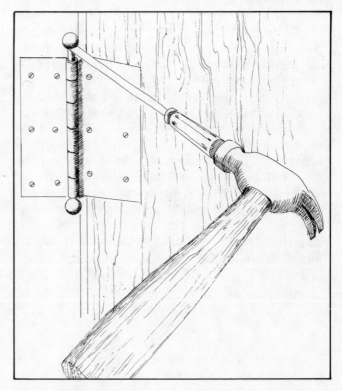

Remove door hinges.

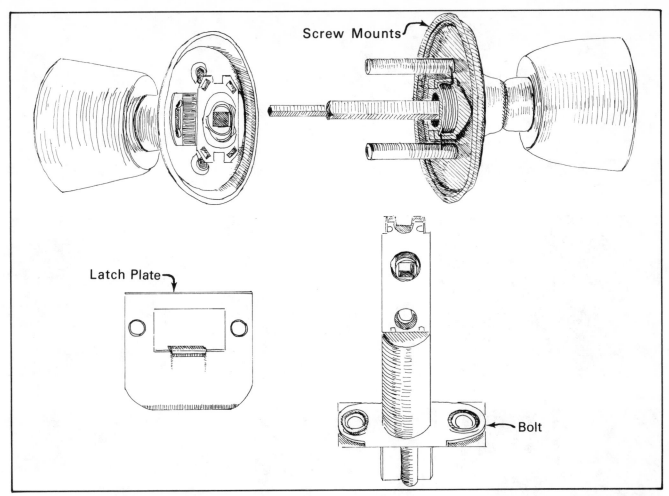

Screw Mounts

Latch Plate

Bolt

Just follow the instructions on the new lockset, or study the old before replacing it. They look much more compli- *cated than they really are. Shown above are lockset components.*

This repair should last as long as the original wood. If the problem reoccurs, repeat the procedure.

Stripped Out Hinge Screws As already explained, fill out the holes by dipping wooden matches liberally into epoxy, jamming them into the holes. Let dry, and cure well. When thoroughly set, break off matches flush, file or sand, and drill small pilot hole and rehang.

If you have no epoxy glue handy, sometimes a simple wooden match jammed into the hole and broken off will do the job temporarily.

Squeaky Hinges Oil, of course, cures squeaky hinges. But oil can be messy and smelly and to avoid the petroleum stink you might try vegetable oil, which works well; or, for a lasting cure pull the hinge pins and wipe them lightly with petroleum jelly. It will last for months or even years, with never a sound.

Loose Hinges When hinges are very old, or have had excessive use, they will often wear themselves "loose" around the hinge pins—the holes actually get larger. The best solution is to replace the whole hinge. But sometimes old hinges are beautiful, and

cannot be replaced.

Still, you cannot have doors rattling and wobbling every time you open them; the cure is to pull the hinge plates and "compress" the pin holes slightly in a vise. Not too much pressure here, just a tiny bit for each of the little hinge pin holes, on both plates for each hinge. Wipe the hinge pin with petroleum jelly and put it all back together. The hinges will last for another five years or so, and should be as tight as new hinges.

Locksets

Replacing Locksets Work with the door open, and look all around the knob until you find a spring slotted lock—just an edge of metal. Push this in with a knifeblade and it will release the knob. Pull the knob off to expose the whole lockset assembly. All this will be on the interior side of the house or locked room, if the lockset was installed correctly.

Two screws will go all the way through the door to hold the assembly in place. Take them out, then pull the assembly out from both sides.

Now go to the edge of the door and you will find

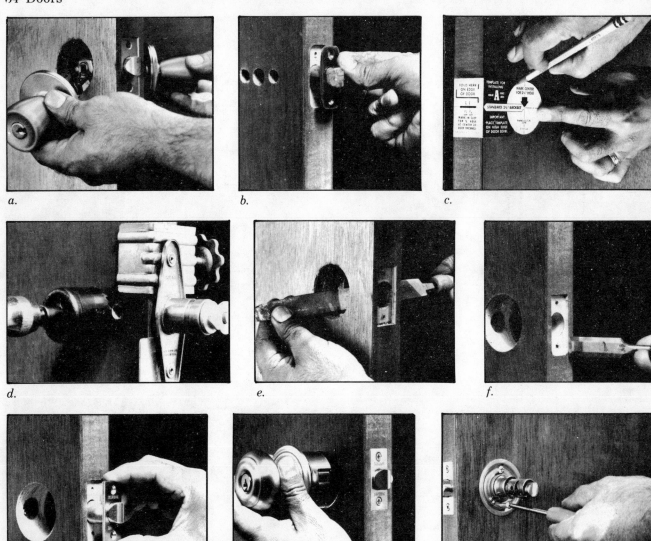

a.

b.

c.

d.

e.

f.

g.

h.

i.

a. Remove worn out, broken, or low-security lock.

b. Remove latch of old lock.

c. Use template packed with new lock to mark area to be enlarged.

d. If a jig is available (as shown), use hole saw to enlarge area to accept new lock mechanism.

e. If hole requires only minor enlargement use a wood rasp or similar tool.

f. Cut away excess wood in edge of door, if necessary, to accommodate new latch plate.

g. Install latch.

h. Insert lock mechanism from outside of door.

i. Attach mounting plate on outside of door and snap on trim and knob.

two small wood screws holding the actual latching mechanism in place. Remove them and pull the latch out.

Installation of the new lockset is a simple reversal of the procedure. Screw the latch in first, then put the lockset assembly in with the key portion facing the outside. With burglary increasing at a drastic rate, remember that a lockset merely keeps the door closed, and is not adequate to stop entry. It is so easily slipped open that even children can pop a lockset.

Chain slide locks are not secure for anything other than mental reassurance. Anybody can kick a door open and tear off the chain lock in the process.

Most authorities recommend that for relative security you need a dead-bolt kind of system, either the over-and-down manual or key-driven bolt that actually goes from the door over *into* the door frame and seats in metal.

Installing such a bolt lock set is easy—they come with precut templates and complete instructions.

Rough-Working Locksets Especially with newer homes, but now and then with older homes, the locksets will work only with difficulty and require much key wiggling.

The classic fix is to squirt a bit of graphite lubricant into the keyhole; usually it will work well enough. But if along with the graphite you take some steel wool and work the teeth on the keyhole down so they are not rough, you will find that it works much better.

Freeing Up Old Locksets A major problem with old homes is that their truly beautiful locksets—sometimes of ornate bronze, or sculpted leaf patterns—do not work. They have rusted or corroded into uselessness.

Of course for security purposes, as already discussed, you should put in a decent dead-bolt system anyway. But even so, it is sometimes nice to have the old one work—at least the latch part, if only for looks.

The best way to free up the lockset is to remove it and clean off the dirt or rust. First take the knobs off, then the pull-out square rod that holds the knobs, and finally the two cover plates. Soak the whole thing in some loosening-solvent product that you can buy in any hardware store. Let it soak for a few days, until all the rust and dirt has loosened, and all the screws and pieces work easily. Then rinse it in thin motor oil, let it hang for another day, wipe it well with clean dry rags, and put it back on the door exactly the same as it came out. Some of those old sets were virtually custom-made for the door; often they will only fit one way, with the screws going back on exactly as they came out.

Do not drown everything with oil. Be sure it has been wiped well before installing because the oil can stain the door around the lockset.

Too Tight or Too Loose?

Sticking Doors The most common door problem is sticking. The door that jams and will not open without that extra tug is especially frustrating.

There are several reasons for a door sticking, and because of that you should do nothing when a door first begins to stick. You must watch and further evaluate the situation.

The cause of the door's sticking might be critical. Often, for instance, doors stick because humidity has risen and caused the wood to swell. This problem is easily fixed, as will be discussed shortly. If it is due to a temporary weather condition such as a rainstorm that has moved in or a pressure system bringing a sudden and unusual increase in humidity, leave the door alone. The condition will pass and the door will return to normal.

Now and again, however, the sticking door merely signals some other underlying problem. If the house sags, for example, it can throw out door frames all over the house. The first indication you will have is

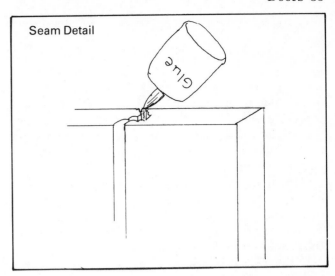

Work the glue deeply into the seams.

Let door rest on floor using pencils as spacers and supports.

Twist the rope tight enough to squeeze out excess glue, but not so tight that the rope breaks.

the sudden sticking of doors where they once moved freely.

If a door or doors begin to stick, look closely at the house particularly in the basement beneath the sticking door if possible. See if there is any evidence of sag—split boards, cracked drywall or plaster. It is treatable even if it is a sagging wall (caused by water problems, termites, rot), but you should know the condition and cause of the difficulty before attempting repair.

If the house does not sag and the humidity has not suddenly risen, still do not take action until you check the door frame. The frames of the door may have shrunk, pulled in from their nails, and effectively made the doorway smaller.

If the frame has shrunk, take a hammer and, using a buffer board to pound on while keeping the door open, go down both sides of the doorway opening, pounding the jamb outwards, stopping to pound every six inches or so.

If the door moves freely after this, take some 10d finishing nails and nail the jamb firmly in position. Then set the nails and fill the holes with a stick of appropriately colored nail filler material. If your home has reoccurring high humidity—due for example to a new humidifier or plants in the room— and the door is likely to stay swollen, it will have to be pulled and wood taken off.

Here again, it is best to stay away from the time-honored method. For decades, any time a door has stuck, the homeowner has jerked it down and planed a bit off the edge to make it fit. Well, this will work. But planes are tricky; if the blade is set wrong or you hit the grain wrong it is possible to mar the edge of the door.

It is better to set the door up on edge and use a non-filling wood rasp to take off about a sixteenth of an inch. The rasp will not "run away" with you and split the wood out; it will just take off a little with each sweep, and leave you in control.

Take off a touch more than you think you will need to take off, to make it loose; then paint or varnish the edge of the door to match and rehang the door, using sticks or pencils to hold it in position.

Shrunken Door Panels Almost the opposite of the swelling, sticking door, shrinking usually occurs with new panelled doors; these panels can shrink a great deal. The cause is too green a wood used in construction, a side effect of trying to produce homes as quickly and therefore as cheaply as possible. It is not uncommon to find bare wood showing around a painted panel. This strip can be as much as ¼ inch, and can be pretty unsightly.

Unfortunately there is no way to "cure" the problem, short of returning the door to the manufacturer.

All you can do is paint the offending strip of wood to match, using paint or stain. And if the panel has become loose, so it rattles in its slot, squirt just a little glue back into the crack; the white glue in the squeeze bottle will work well.

Separation of Corners One of the primary problems with older doors is that the members come apart. The glue dries out, the weather comes in and the door literally begins to fall apart.

Take the door down, but not apart, work a good wood glue deeply into the seams between the members and press them back together. Take a piece of inexpensive hemp rope ½ inch in diameter, and make a tourniquet clamp as illustrated.

When the wood has been tightened enough to be firm and squeeze the glue out of the cracks, wipe excess glue off and tie or tape the stick of your clamp in position until the glue is well dried.

Do not try to hurry this process. Let the glue dry completely, perhaps for a couple of days, before rehanging the door.

Latches

Stripped Out Latch Screws As with hinge screws, the screws holding the latch set in the door or wall can strip out. Mix a little epoxy and jam it back into the hole with a wooden match.

When the epoxy is well set (some of the new so-called five minute epoxies are very good for this), break the matches off flush and sand level before rescrewing the latch back in.

Rotted-Out Latch Assemblies Older homes frequently will have the latch assemblies rotted out of the exterior doors due to bad weather and poor maintenance.

Replacing the door is expensive and often it is impossible to find a new door as suited to the house as the old one. As an alternative, you can "rebuild" the latch hole and make it serve for years.

Start with rubber gloves, and then mix a putty of epoxy and wood sanding dust. Mix it with a flat knife or wooden match and keep adding sanding dust until you have a thickish putty that will hold a shape. You can get the sanding dust by sanding a soft pine scrap with coarse sandpaper.

Once the putty has thickened and the latch assembly has been removed from the door, clean out all split and rotted wood from the hole. Rebuild it to the original shape using the epoxy-wood putty.

Do not use quick-dry epoxy. Use the slow-drying epoxy and take your time. Just fill and push so that the epoxy works well back into the damaged wood, and build it out until the repair job approximates the original shape. Let it cure for two or three days; really let it set up before replacing the lockset.

All pilot holes for screws should be drilled smaller than if you were using natural wood, but do not worry about holding power—the epoxy will hold well because the wood sandings give it tensile strength. Also, we attempted to fix a rotted door using premixed fiberglass putty; theoretically it would work well for this application. But it did not turn out well at all. The material seemed too brittle.

Doors That Will Not Latch After a time some doors stop latching correctly; old doors kind of half catch, then swing open.

The cause is age again—the casing shrinks until the latch plate in the casing actually moves too far away from the door for the latch to engage it properly. What you have to do, obviously, is move the latch plate back over so the latch will catch it and lock.

There are several ways of doing this, including shimming out with wood, as most people do. But if you take an old piece of thick boot leather, cut it the same size as the latch plate and put it beneath the plate for a shim, not only will you find it easier to use than wood but it will not split out.

Trim off any excess with a razor blade and touch up the edge of leather with appropriate paint or varnish. The leather takes stain and looks like wood when you are finished.

General Problems

Rehanging Doors Putting a door back on after repairing it is relatively simple if you do not try to lift the whole door by one corner.

Put some pencils or pieces of wood of the same thickness across the door jamb, and rehanging the door will be easy.

Screws Coming Loose Because of heavy use, wood screws often work loose. When this happens, pull them and give them a covering of glue. Then screw them back in while the glue is still wet, and it should solve the problem.

Sliding Doors

Rough Track Movement Almost all problems with sliding doors come down to dirty tracks. Any time a sliding door does not work properly, first check the bottom slide track for obstructions. Usually you will find something jammed into the track as though it had been welded there.

If the bottom track is clear, check the top for possible obstructions. If both tracks are clear, check the wheel adjustment screws located at the bottom corners. They sometimes vibrate loose with use and allow the door to "settle" too far down on the track for easy movement.

If the tracks are not obstructed, and the screws have not come loose, check to see if the house is settling. On a span as wide as a sliding glass door a little settling in the middle can have a very noticeable effect on the door movement. A half inch or so can warp the frame so badly the door will be almost impossible to open or close.

If the house has settled check the chapter on "Aging" for possible repairs. Do not try to adjust the door enough to compensate for a continuing sag; you will not be able to keep up with the sag and the effect will be that the doors look crooked and strange.

Rough Latches It is almost impossible to find a sliding glass door with a latch that does work correctly.

To repair, fill the offending latch with graphite lubricant and pray for the best. Generally, over a period of time and with additional use and graphite, the action will smooth out. With sliding door systems the way they are now, that is about all you can hope for. Replacing the door may solve it, but the percentages are that a new door will also have a rough-working latch. New sliding glass doors can be bought in preassembled packages with complete instructions for homeowner installation.

Plumbing and Water Appliances

Major plumbing repairs, when replumbing of a whole house is necessary due to pipe rot, for example, are very difficult and should not be attempted without a thorough knowledge of both the tools, the materials, and the system. It demands strength and is dirty work.

With the question of major problems out of the way it might be salient to point out that in all other cases repairs are simple, if sometimes a bit noxious, and are within reach of the homeowner. If a certain degree of care is taken the home repair will be of professional quality.

Drains

Far and away the most common plumbing problem is the stopped drain.

First, try the plunger. Push down and pull up with surging action to try to blow a "plug" of water through the stopped area. Usually this will work. After the drain is cleared, run very hot water through it. Often the plug will consist of grease or sludge buildup and hot water will melt the grease out and completely clean the pipe. Aside from television ads, no consistent success is apparent using various drain cleaning agents, either liquid or granular. On a maintenance basis they may work, but for cleaning a really stopped drain they never seem to get the job done.

If the plunger does not work, find the easiest access point and go down through the sink drain or toilet with a long piece of wire. It is possible the plugged area is close and the wire will work through. Again, if the wire clears the drain, run hot water through it and bore it out.

If the wire does not work, use a snake—the wire-coil kind used by plumbers. They can be rented, if you do not own one or know where to borrow one. Work the snake into the easiest access point that is relatively straight; do not go through the trap, but below the trap once it has been removed. The less bends you have to negotiate, the better. Wear gloves and gently work the snake down to the stopped point, then back and forth until you break through. Never force anything, but move back and forth, back and forth, until the resistance is gone. If you keep pushing the plug blockage—and in an old house it could be fifteen feet of solid materials—it will just compact and form a more solid front. You must allow the snake to find a way through, a bit at a time. When the drain is cleared run hot water through to further open it.

Leaking Drains In plumbing problems a leak almost always means either a broken pipe or loose joint. Under-sink leaks are the most common and they usually come from traps. The most common

PLUMBING TROUBLE-SHOOTING CHART
DRAINS

Symptoms	Main drain backup	Main drain, yard	Clogged traps	Using plunger	Using wire	Using snake	Using hose, basement	Septic system	Treating clogged drain at same level
Sink backing up			X	X	X	X		X	
Tub backing up			X	X	X			X	
Toilet backing up	X			X					X
Water backing up in basement	X	X			X	X	X		
Water backing up (seepage) in yard	X						X		
Water backing up (dripping) in basement ceiling		X						X	
Water on upstairs floor								X	
Water under cabinets in kitchen/bathroom		X						X	
Seepage (dampness) around house		X						X	
Turn to repair info on ...	Main drain backup	Main drain, yard	Clogged traps	Using plunger	Using wire	Using snake	Using hose, basement	Septic system	Treating clogged drain at same level

cause of traps that leak is worn ring-washers at the joints. Repair is easy, but messy. Use a large pipe wrench and loosen the big nuts at either end of the trap—after positioning a pot or bucket to catch the inevitable water. Wiggle and pull the trap out of place and remove the mashed washers around the ends. They will be almost flat, and possibly torn. Take them to the local hardware store, buy new ones, and put the whole assembly back together. When retightening the nuts do not go overboard with the wrench. You can develop a lot of torque with a large pipe wrench and the threads are easy to strip. Just get it snug-tight and let it go at that.

If the source of the drain leak is not in the trap, but is further down the line, the repair depends on the kind of pipe. If you have threaded, galvanized pipe for a drain system, common in older homes, take a large pipe wrench, adjust it to fit tight until the teeth will bite in, and tighten the leaking pipe a quarter turn. Use plenty of force. Old pipes are very hard to move. But do not overdo it. A drip-leak will be cured with just a little tightening: all that is necessary is enough pressure to recompress the loosened threads inside the pipe. The leak results when corrosion slightly erodes the threads and allows a trickle of water to work through; the slightest tightening will stop the leak and retighten the corroded spot.

If the leaking drain comes from a plastic pipe, more common in newer homes, just put a dab of plastic pipe adhesive at the leak point. Allow it to dry for a few minutes before using it. If you do not have any plastic pipe adhesive, a model airplane cement will do the job.

Very rarely a drain leak will occur in a copper drain pipe. This is rare because copper is very expensive and not often used in drains. If a leak occurs at a solder joint, use a small propane torch to heat the leak area. Heat just until the solder begins to flow, then instantly remove the heat. It is not necessary to add solder; just heat the existing solder to fill the gap.

The final drain leak covered here occurs around a cast pipe, usually in the basement, where the pipe goes down the wall or into the floor. Here the packing might come loose around a joint where two sections of cast pipe come together. Take a screwdriver and hammer and repack the joint. This leak is uncommon because the packing does not usually come loose, and even if it does the leak will not show unless a plug backs the drain up enough to force the water back out.

In all drain leak problems, try not to hurry. Often, especially in small drip-leaks or seepage problems, the drain will fix itself.

Fixing pipes or drains is not as complicated as it looks.

Pipes

One of the most common leak problems is the dripping faucet. Usually, the drip occurs when the rubber washer in the tip of the assembly wears down. The washer is on the faucet handle, attached to the end by a little screw. Buy a box of assorted rubber faucet washers at a hardware store, just to have on hand, and make sure you have a small pipe wrench and a good screwdriver.

Under the sink you will find two secondary gate valves—faucet handles—first you turn these off. This prevents additional water from coming into the pipe. Then you turn the leaking faucets on, to release pressure, and when no more water is running, remove the faucet handle. You will note that the faucet is held down in the housing by a standard collar-nut. Use the pipe wrench to loosen this nut, by turning it counterclockwise, and when it has been removed the faucet core will lift out of the housing. On the bottom of the faucet core there is a rubber washer; take the screw out and replace it with the right-sized washer from the assorted washer box. Then reverse the process, putting the core back in, the collar-nut on and the handle back on. The leak will have stopped dripping.

Galvanized-Pipe Leaks Seep-drip leaks in exposed pipes, as with drain repair, depend on the type

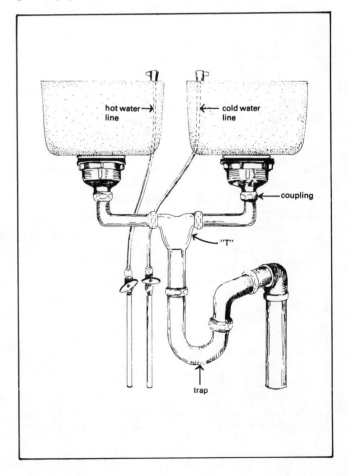

hot water line

cold water line

coupling

"T"

trap

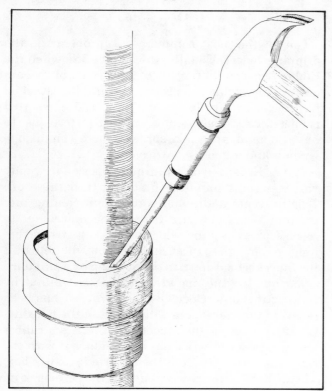

Drive the lead and packing down hard to seal the joint, then look for the cause of the drain backing up to stop the joint leak at its source.

house (usually in the basement) and allow all the water in the pipes to drain down and out. Also open up an upstairs faucet to allow air to bleed down into the pipe when the water runs out; this will ensure a thorough drain.

With the pipes drained, repair can be started. If the leak is plastic, work some plastic adhesive into the hole and allow it to dry well for over an hour before putting pressure on the pipe again. Unlike drain situations, here there will be a significant amount of pressure, perhaps forty to sixty psi, so be sure the fix has taken effect before restoring water.

If the slow leak is in copper pipe, the most common in relatively recent homes, the first step is the same. Turn off the water, drain all the pipes, then use a propane torch to heat the leaking joint to allow the solder to reform. As with drains it is not necessary to apply more solder.

Finally, discussing slow leaks, be sure that the problem is indeed a leak. Sometimes a change in atmospheric conditions will cause a pipe to "sweat" and leave a few drops. Be certain the pipe is leaking, and that a bit of condensation hasn't just formed.

Burst Pipes Generally caused by freezing, and most often in hot-water heating systems which have been left untended for a few days or weeks, burst pipes can involve extensive household damage if not caught immediately.

A frozen pipe will stay plugged until it melts out. But once it melts and starts to allow water to flow, the leak may ruin walls, ceilings, and floors.

The repair need not be costly if caught in time. First, obviously, you must turn off the source of water. As quickly as you find the burst pipe, turn off the main water to the house and open a lower faucet or drain to relieve the pressure in the broken area.

When all water is drained out of the pipe, a further more detailed evaluation is necessary. Specific repair methods depend on the kind of pipe involved.

If galvanized, use a large pipe wrench to break loose and unscrew the section of pipe that has burst.

of pipe. If the leaking pipes are galvanized, just tighten the leaking joint a hair with a pipe wrench (not over a quarter turn). As with drains, the threads rust and corrode. If you recompress them a bit the leak is fixed.

Nongalvanized-Pipe Leaks Whenever the pipe does not have threaded joints the pipe should be drained of water to repair a slow or seeping leak.

Find the main gate valve for the house. Somewhere in the basement, crawl space, or just outside, there will be a single faucet handle that cuts off water to the whole house. Turn the water off with this main valve, then open the lowest faucet in the

PLUMBING TROUBLE-SHOOTING CHART LEAKS						
Symptoms						
Faucet drip	X					
Dampness on floor			X	X		
Spray leak		X		X		X
Flow leak		X		X		X
Seep leak			X	X		
Burst leak				X		X
"Puddling" around faucet mount	X				X	
Turn to repair info on . . .	Replacing faucet washer	Stopping leak with epoxied screw	Condensation	Leak repairs	Main faucet repacking	Shutting water at main in basement

Take out the whole piece, even if it is long. Remember that it unscrews like a regular bolt: counterclockwise to loosen, clockwise to tighten. Before breaking it loose find the nearest coupling joint and release that end at the coupling by unscrewing it. Holding the burst piece of galvanized pipe, go to the local plumbing supply or hardware store and get a piece of new pipe that is cut to the right length and threaded the same as the one you have taken out. While you are there pick up a tube of pipe compound to smear on the threads.

Back at the house, smear all the threads with the pipe compound and rebuild the damaged section of pipe with the new pipe making everything as tight as you can. When you think the pipe is repaired turn the water on and see what happens. There might be a small seep leak. If so, just tighten a little to further compress the threads and swage the goop in.

If the burst pipe is plastic, repair is easy. After the water system is turned off and drained, cut out the broken piece of tubing with a hacksaw. Then get a new, exactly-the-same-size piece from the hardware store and a couple of slip-couplings plus a small can of plastic pipe adhesive. First put the couplings on the two ends of the cut off pipes in the wall, gluing them liberally and allowing the glue to dry. Put a good coat of glue on both ends of the new piece of pipe and work it into the two couplings. After it dries

well, over an hour, hit it with water pressure. If there is a seep leak (unlikely), turn off the water, drain the system again and apply more glue to the leak.

If the burst pipe is copper, which is the most likely, the repair is again relatively simple. Drain the system and use a hacksaw to cut out the broken piece of pipe, going well back on both sides of the burst area to get completely free of the swelling.

Then get a propane torch, a small can of flux and a small roll of solder wire (the kind for plumbing). Along with these items buy a new piece of the right-diameter copper pipe, cut to fit in the place the old came out, and two slip-coupling tubes and a piece of fine emery paper.

First use the emery paper and sand the places where all the pipes will come together. Just abrade

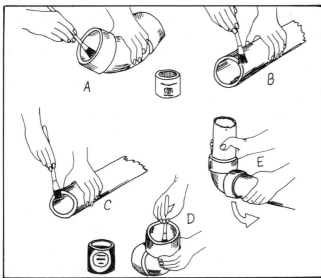

Joining DWV Plastic Pipe can be accomplished in just a few steps with a brush. First, the bed of the plastic pipe socket is brushed with a cleaning agent (A); same is done for the outer rim of the pipe to be inserted (B). Next, a special welding solvent is brushed on the pipe rim (C) and inner side of socket (D). The joint is then completed by simply inserting the pipe in the fitting Socket (E) with a tightening, twisting motion.

Sockets are provided on all fittings, which come in a full range of types including a splicing collar. Plastic pipe comes in plain 10 foot lengths, and is cut to proper length for use with an ordinary carpenter's handsaw.

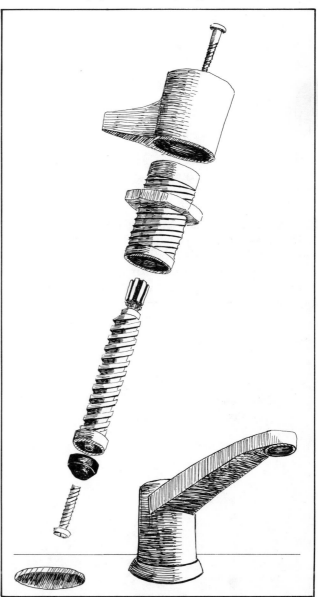

The washer is at the very bottom of the assembly. One nice feature is that faucets usually come apart easily because they are used so much.

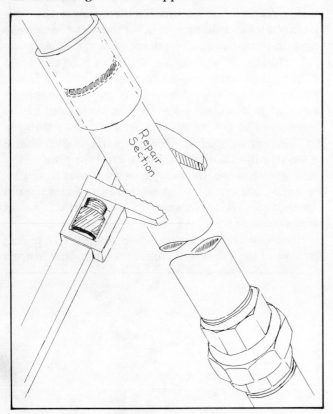

Use plenty of heft when wrenching loose galvanized pipes. They are usually nearly welded shut with rust and age.

with the brush provided in the flux can. Do *no* soldering or heating at this time; just flux and build the whole repair in place.

When complete and in place use the propane torch, to "spray" heat the joints one at a time. Play the flame gently back and forth, holding the torch back three or four inches from the copper. Keep touching the joint area with the solder wire as you heat the copper. At a certain point you will note that the solder becomes melted by the copper, not by the torch. At the same moment it will "flow," actually seem to run of its own volition back into the seam between the coupling and the pipe. Right then, when it runs or flows, run the wire end of the solder around the joint so a good load of solder goes back into the seam between the coupling and the pipe. Not a large amount—just a bit—and then back off by pulling the propane and solder away immediately. Allow it to cool, then do the same to the other end of the same coupling. Allow that to cool, then go the other end of the pipe and repeat, one coupling seam at a time. Once the repair is finished and it has cooled for a while, turn the water on. There probably will not be a leak, but if there is turn everything off, redrain the system and repeat the soldering process at the leak area. Do not overdo it, but heat the pipe until the solder runs, then back off; it should not take very much to fix the remaining leak.

The most common area for a burst or frozen pipe is in a hot-water heating system. Usually this happens when the house is untended and the boiler goes out for one reason or another. And most often the break will occur inside one of the heating units, back in a low corner where the cold settles first.

them enough to shine them up and clean them. When they are all sanded use the externals of the pipes and internals of the slip coupling tubes to "build" the repair section in place. Apply flux to each joint as you put the pipe together, wiping well

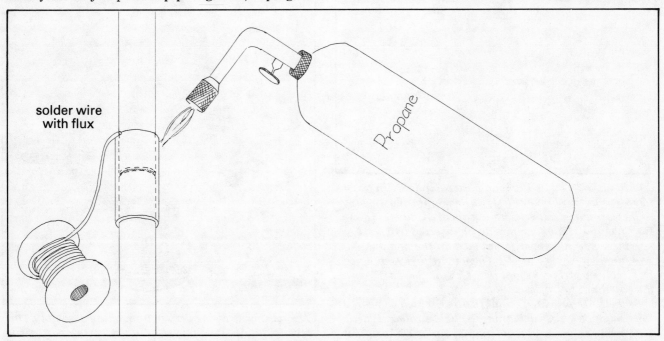

solder wire with flux

Propane

Gently "spray" heat the joints one at a time, touching   solder wire to the joint area as you heat the pipe.

The repair is the same as just described. The only difference is that the copper pipe is inside the heater housing on the baseboard. Take off the housing and then remove the radiation fins; the fins are easily taken off the break area. The copper pipe is cut out the same as in straight-pipe cases, and the couplings soldered in place. Then leave the fins off when done; they will not fit well once the couplings are soldered and may prevent heat distribution. This will not greatly impair the efficiency of the unit.

Catastrophic leaks that are hidden inside walls or ceilings require that the wall or ceiling be torn apart, the leak area exposed, the leak repaired; then the walls or ceiling are repaired as per methods explained in the appropriate chapter in this book.

Hot-Water Heaters— Gas and Electric

The only thing that goes wrong with a hot-water heater is that it lets the water get cold. Gas heaters go out and electric heaters trip breakers.

For relighting gas heaters, follow the instructions on the little panel over the control opening that goes into the burner. They are usually very explicit, but it helps to hold the reset button on the pilot light down for a full minute or longer.

Electric hot-water heaters will have a "reset" button somewhere. Find it, hold it in per instructions, and the heater will come back on. If not, and if the main breakers are not popped, the element might be burned out. These unscrew, pull straight out, and can be replaced by going to the appropriate dealer. Drop a new one in, screw the wires back on and hit the breaker which you had turned off for safety before starting.

Leaks around pipes coming out of hot-water heaters should be repaired the same as regular pipe leaks. Just remember to let everything cool down in order to avoid burning your hands, and drain the system through the lowest drain. Also remember to turn the heating element, gas or electric, off.

Wells and Septic Systems

While not specifically having to do with plumbing, wells and septic systems fit best into this category.

Wells With wells, and speaking from a strictly repair standpoint, there is relatively little that can be home repaired. Problems with wells tend to be major—polluted water, blown submerged pumps (by lightning), shifted and broken casings; none of the real problems with wells lend themselves to easy home repair. Often heavy equipment is needed to pull the well, or special purifying machinery is required. This type of work is beyond most home-owners.

Still, there are a few things that happen that can be "fixed" at home. First, a common mistake in working with wells is to overemphasize the problem. Do not jump to the expensive conclusion but check out the easy solution first. If the well suddenly stops, for instance, it does not necessarily mean the pump is blown. Check the power supply; make sure it is not just a breaker or fuse popped by a temporary overload condition, which is very common and usually the trouble. If everything seems normal, look for "hidden" safety systems. Quite often, as an example, there will be an overload breaker on the pressure tank or near the pressure switching system. Here again, a temporary surge or condition may have tripped the switch and caused the well to stop pumping. Be sure to reset all switches and replace all fuses before calling in outside help. If the breaker trips repeatedly, or fuses keep blowing, then the problem is more complicated and will require knowledgeable help.

Under no condition should you take chances with your health and your water supply. If you suspect that the water has gone bad or changed; if there is just a faint new odor or strange taste; stop drinking the water at once. Take a sample to the county health board and get it analyzed. It will not take long and costs little or nothing.

Septic Systems If a septic system is put in properly and a tile field well laid out and installed, there is very little that can go wrong. With normal use, and a moderate approach to water-dumping appliances like dishwashers, a good septic system will last virtually forever.

When they go bad it usually is because the system was not made right in the first place, and the symptom is inevitably that the tank and/or tile field overflows and allows raw sewage to come out on the lawn. Or the basement drain backs up and does not respond to treatment with a plumbing snake.

Proper repair involves redigging and relaying the field, after probably blasting it with dynamite to "loosen" the base rock and soil. It is as complicated, difficult and dangerous as it sounds.

If it is necessary to tear the septic out or the yard is damaged, you will find that new grass really *does* grow wildly over the septic. Just rake and reseed and *do not* fertilize. If you have to fill with dirt and are wondering how to quickly calculate the amount of dirt to order in cubic yards, just remember that a space three feet by three feet on the sides and one foot deep equals a third of a "yard" (a cubic yard is 27 cubic feet). Somehow it is not as hard to visualize a third—three-by-three by one foot thick—of a cubic yard whereas a whole one is hard to measure in your mind. Any extra, hold and use to fill in as the new soil settles and compacts. Order about ten percent extra to be safe.

It is possible, however, to effect at least a temporary kind of "repair" without going through the trouble of getting in heavy equipment and tearing the yard apart.

If your septic system begins to come out the top, vastly curtail the use of your drain system for a couple of weeks. Stop using the dishwasher, likewise the clothes washer (go to the laundromat), and cut down on the number of showers. No baths; they use too much water. What you're doing is cutting down the intake completely to the tank and tile field and allowing the ground to dry out; quite literally giving the earth a rest.

Very often this rest and rejuvenation period will be enough to allow the system to return to normal.

If just backing off does not "repair" the septic system, the problems are more severe. A spring may have started feeding into the tile field or a pipe may have burst—and there is no home remedy that will work.

Sometimes septics quit "working". The tank no longer functions in a bacterial sense and does not work the solids down to a liquid that the tile field can handle. This might be noted by the system backing up, but more often it will be a smell that *cannot* be ignored.

Toilet Repairs

Chipped Enamel Use a liquid porcelain glaze patching compound for chips. Badly cracked toilet fixtures cannot be repaired and should be replaced.

Fiberglass Surfaces Never use scouring powders or pads on a fiberglass surface. Minor stains and cigarette burns can be removed by rubbing lightly with 600 grit sandpaper and a small amount of scouring powder. Repolish with automotive wax.

Mechanical Problems Leaks, squeaks, and whistles are caused by a water supply that does not shut off or an outlet valve that does not close—or both. Mechanisms within the water tanks vary but are designed to produce enough water for thorough flushing. They can be replaced within a minute or so. The accompanying sketch of the most common mechanism found within a water closet shows what should happen when you push the handle to flush the toilet. The rod attached to the handle lifts the tank ball, opens the outlet, and permits water to flow into the toilet bowl. The tank ball then falls back into place, closing the outlet; the tank is refilled from the inlet tube. As the water refills the tank it raises the float ball, which measures the water and closes the supply valve at the proper level.

If water continues to run into the bowl, some part of the mechanism is out of order. Leaks are usually caused by improper seating of the tank ball. Check to see that the ball wire and rod guide are not bent. Or there could a worn washer in the intake valve. To replace this washer you will have to remove a lever; remember to shut off the water supply to the tank before beginning.

The "plumber's helper" or plunger is usually the first attempt in fixing a clogged toilet. However, instead of the bulb-type suction-cup style used for sinks, you need a molded-force-ball type that exerts a lot more pressure. Leave several inches of water in the toilet bowl and insert the plunger into the opening. Start pumping. If the plunger does not handle the repair, you may need a closet auger to break loose the obstruction. If this does not work, the toilet will have to be removed from the floor.

Installing Toilet Tank and Bowl The first requirement is a thoroughly clean floor surface where the toilet will be located. Then follow these steps or the instructions supplied by the manufacturer.

• Place the fixture upside down on a protective soft material to prevent scratching, and apply a warmed wax ring to the circular recess at the base of the bowl. The fixture will be connected to the waste line through this recess. Then apply a setting compound to the outer rim of the bowl to assure a continuous seal to the floor.

• Set the bowl carefully atop the metal flange already attached on the floor. The toilet bolts fit through the holes in the base of the fixture, ready to receive washers and nuts. Tighten these snugly, but do not force-tighten or you will strip the threads.

Following placement of large donut-shaped washers on the threaded tank outlet, place the tank on the ledge of the bowl and align for placement of bolts downward through the bolt holes of the two parts. Again, the bolts should be tightened carefully, alternating from side to side to prevent breaking the tank or bowl.

• The cold-water line must then be connected to the tank with a straight or angle stop. Now you can insert the ballcock into the tank and secure it in position. This mechanism varies according to the unit purchased, so read installation instructions on the package.

Turn water on by opening the angle or straight stop located beneath the tank. The tank should fill to the "water line" indicated inside the tank. If it does not, the brass rod supporting the ball float should be bent until the tank stops filling at the water line.

More details on toilet repair and installation can be found in *Bathroom Planning and Remodeling* and *Homeowners Guide to Plumbing*.

Leaky flush valves attributable to a conventional toilet tank mechanism can be eliminated with a Flusher Fixer Kit available from hardware and lumber dealers. The kit replaces the worn-out tank ball or flapper and does away with lift wires and brackets that often become bent. Unlike conventional flush valve assemblies, the kit is installed without tools and without removing the tank from the bowl. The kit's seat is simply bonded directly onto the existing seat with a patented watertight sealant.

The old tank stopper ball is first removed from the toilet along with the lift wires and bracket guide. Steel wool is then used to clean off the old brass flush valve seat and water used to rinse the seat clean. Waterproof sealant is applied to the underside of the new stainless steel ring using the entire contents of the tube supplied with the kit.

After placement of the new seat on the old brass seat, a 9-ounce can is placed atop the unit to apply necessary bonding weight. The seat is allowed to set in this position for two hours with water level just enough to cover the top rim of the seat. A chain is then secured to the flush valve and attached to the lift arm. Excess chain may be cut off or fastened to the clip, and the toilet is ready to use.

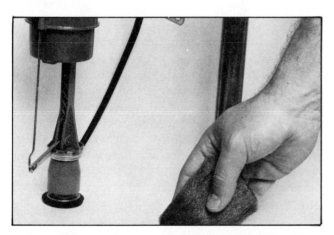

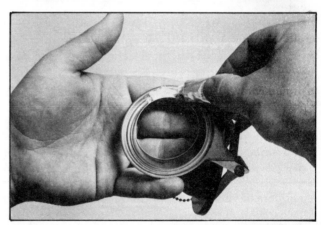

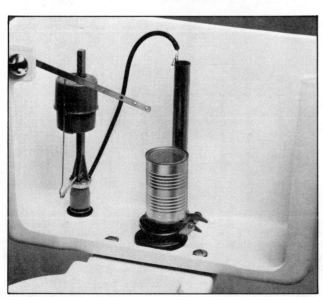

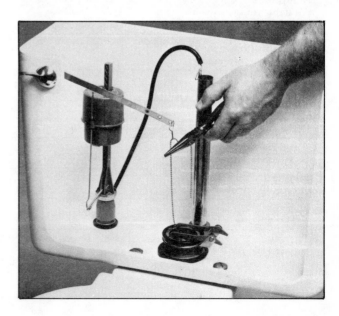

First, at some point in dealing with household electrical difficulties the work becomes a life-threatening job. Extreme caution should be used at all times.

There are several very important facts to remember when considering electrical problems, points so vital that they must be stressed at the outset.

- Never touch a wire you suspect to be hot.
- Never put anything but the accepted type of plug into an outlet.
- Never bypass safety equipment like fuses or appliance interlocks.
- Never hurry.
- Never work beyond your knowledge; if you do not know what you are doing, stop.
- Never take any chances—do not for instance, even touch a power tool if you are standing in water.

The other thing you must remember about electricity is that—with the exception of lightning—there are no "surprises" in electrical problems. If a fuse blows or a circuit breaker pops, it is most definitely because something caused an overload on the line. And if you replace the fuse or reset the breaker and it happens again, you have a problem that cannot be wished away. This will take on more importance as you get into specific repair methods.

For some reason people insist that there are weird "temporary" difficulties that appear and then disappear in electrical systems. Or they do not believe the external indications they see; they continue to ignore popped fuses and breakers and try to work around them.

Overload—Tripped Breaker or Fuse

This situation is the most common electrical problem for the homeowner. It means that something on the line, something in the home, has demanded more power than the system is capable of furnishing safely. In the case of a circuit breaker, a heat-sensing switch has opened and killed the power supply; in the case of a blown fuse a thin strip of metal has melted (literally) and broken the circuit. In either case, the power is cut off and the actual cause could be almost anything.

For that reason the best repair method might be called the ever-more-complicated approach. Start with the simplest possible cause—a temporary line surge in current tripped the breaker. This is rarely the case, however, since electrical power is usually more reliable than that. Still, it is worth checking.

Always try resetting the breaker first. Wait a few moments until it has cooled, then reset or replace the fuse. If that works, you have achieved the simplest repair possible.

ELECTRICAL TROUBLE-SHOOTING CHART
BASIC PROBLEMS

Symptoms	Breakers, fuses in main box	Power outage, call electric company	Calling to check on excess power (surge on the line)	Checking for plug and cord	Checking device in different outlets	Checking for bad appliance or tool (cut power to room with odor)
All lights and power out	X	X				
Lights out to one room	X					
Dim lights (low or slow operation of appliances)		X				
Persistently blowing fuse or popping breaker			X		X	X
High power bills						
Burnt smell in air						X
Warm feeling on wall near outlet						X
Inoperative appliance or tool, TV, or stereo				X	X	
Flickering or blinking lights		X				
Turn to repair info on ...	Breakers, fuses in main box	Power outage, call electric company	Calling to check on excess power (surge on the line)	Checking for plug and cord	Checking device in different outlets	Checking for bad appliance or tool (cut power to room with odor)

If it does not work, widen your scope of inquiry and go to the next-most-complicated possible cause. Remember, something *made* the breaker trip. It also would help if you went around the room or area without power, and listed the appliances that were plugged in at the time. Then add up the watts and you may have your answer without further ado. Most lines will not service more than 2200 watts. Or consider whether you have recently plugged in a light or an appliance on the line. Whatever the size, this recent additional load could be causing the overload. Unplug it, try resetting again, and see whether or not the overload has disappeared.

If you are still faced with loss of power, advance to the next-most-difficult-to-verify possibility: Has some piece of older equipment on the line, such as a light or appliance, suddenly gone bad?

Begin repair by unplugging appliances controlled by that breaker or fuse; take everything external off the line. When it is clear except for built-in lights, hit the breaker again. It will probably hold this time because appliances are generally the cause of tripped fuses or breakers. Then simply plug them back in one at a time until the culprit trips the breaker. You may be able to choose which appliance should be removed from the line. For example, anything portable may be moved to another line with less demand on it.

If taking all appliances off the line still does not answer your problem, widen the scope once again. Have you, or somebody else, done something recently that might cause the breaker to snap? A new nail accidentally driven into a wire would do it, or a

An electrical service entrance may be overhead or underground. Shown here is a typical entrance enclosure with metal base for an underground service drop. At right, the meter and enclosure cover are in place once the home has been completed.

mower cutting through an outside wire. There is a physical cause for that breaker to trip.

At this point you have reached the juncture where you are involved with life-threatening forces. It is at this stage that exposure to electricity becomes necessary. Up to now it has simply been a matter of plugging and unplugging things.

If the breakers still trip, it is necessary to begin removing outlets and light fixtures on the rare possi-

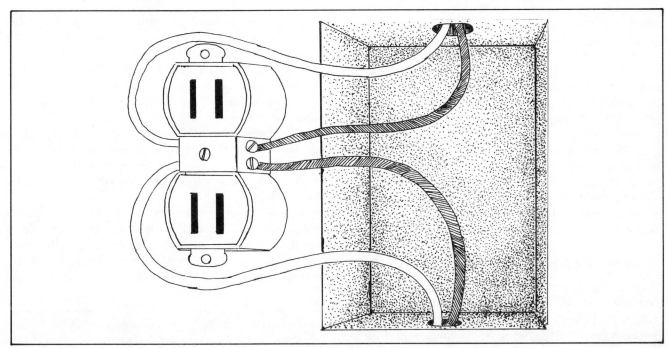

The "guts" of an outlet pulled out, black wires on one side, white on the other. Outlets are not complicated, but be cautious. Remember to always work with power off.

bility that something inside one of them is causing the sudden difficulty.

Caution is the most important element while carrying out this final attempt to solve the problem. Be absolutely positive that all power is off to the house. When you have verified it yourself, then use a screwdriver and remove the cover plate on the first outlet on the circuit that keeps blowing.

With the cover plate off, visually examine the outlet inside. Make certain there are no burned spots, no blown-black carbon areas, assuming it is all clean and clear, do the same with every outlet on the line. Remove all the cover plates and leave them off. Then visually go over them without touching anything to see if you can find some evidence of trouble.

You probably will. Electricity often leaves traces when it gets out of hand. But if you cannot see anything obviously wrong, begin to take the covers off the light fixtures in the ceiling. Just remove the screws and drop all the external covers to check for damage.

If you find either a burnt outlet or light fixture—and keep the power off—remove the outlet or fixture and put a new one in *exactly* the way the old one came out. Put the new black wire where it came off the old one, the new white wire back on the new one exactly as it came off the old, and the new green or bare wire to ground—all just the same. Working with wiring scares some people, but taking out things and putting in the new is really quite simple and basic. Just follow the old pattern exactly; if you have any doubt, draw a quick sketch before you remove the old wiring. All wiring is color-coded—black is power, white neutral, and green or bare wire is the common ground. Draw a small picture showing what colored wires go where, and that will be all you need to know. Nothing is complicated; just do not hurry, and work within your knowledge. If you do something wrong, the worst that should happen is that the breaker will trip when you resupply the power.

A last thought on working this way, in ever-expanding circles: the chances of ever getting to the point of pulling outlets or light fixtures is minimal. This discussion is for methodology, but in virtually all cases the trouble will show itself right away, and will turn out to be an overloaded circuit.

Nonworking Power—No Juice

The second most common electrical problem is lack of power when you plug in an appliance or tool.

Again, the search for the root of the trouble, and method for effecting repair, requires working in expanding circles.

The probable cause is a faulty tool or appliance.

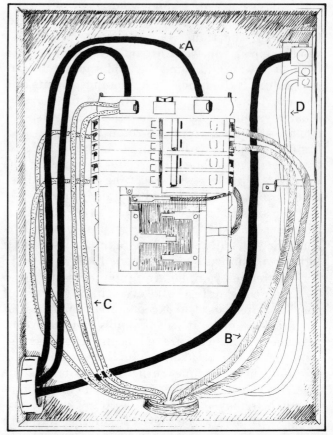

Circuit Breaker Diagram:
A—input from power lines, coming in through transformer;
B—circuit wire throughout house;
C—220 volts to range and appliances;
D—neutral, ground wires.

Quickly grab another tool and plug it into the same outlet to verify whether or not the tool actually works. If the new tool works where the old one did not, then either repair the tool or take it back to the manufacturer; actually, in all cases take it back to the manufacturer. There are far too many substandard tools being built.

In almost all cases the tool or appliance will be the problem rather than the power source. But for purposes of repair methods, let us assume that the tool or appliance is not faulty; the second try does not work either.

Expand the scope of repair work. Go back to the breaker or fuse box and verify that a breaker or fuse has not tripped or burned out. Working with pure probability, usually loss of power is due to a breaker or fuse. Reset and if it does not hold, work it out as an overload problem.

If a rare occasion has come up and the tool is good, and the breaker has not tripped, verify that the house as a whole has power. Make certain that there is electrical power coming in by checking a light or two. Sometimes a power outage will hit during the

1—Unscrew screws holding old switch box.

4—Replace in box.

2—Remove old wires from switch.

5—Add new cover plate.

3—Rewire in new switch.

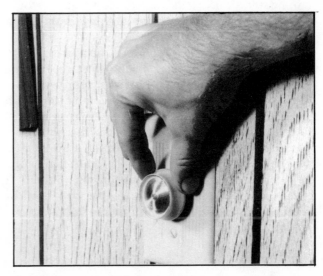

6—And press switch knob in place over spindle.

day and there will be no ready indication, so check around.

If power is available to the house, but still is not going through to the outlets even though you know the breaker is reset, the problem approaches that point where it is perhaps best to call the electrician. Something has caused the wire to open suddenly: the insulation wrapping may be torn, or the wire has been cut or melted itself apart. The repair can be dangerous from the standpoint of the fire precaution and leaking current. When safety becomes a critical issue, it is best to call in outside help.

Nongrounded Circuits or Appliances

Now and then you will experience a mild shock when you touch the sink and an appliance at the same time. This is caused by imperfect grounding of the appliance through the circuits, usually in older homes where there is no ground circuit.

The repair is to use a wire from some metal part of the cover or case—a sheetmetal screw on the back works well—to the nearest proper ground. Just run the wire from a screw to a ground clamp (purchased from the nearest hardware store) on a water pipe, either supply or drain. The ground clamp is cheap and easily installed. You can use any spare electrical wire you can find to do the job. If you haven't any wire, a single strand of 16 gauge wire will do nicely. Strip insulating material from the ends; one end clamps to the appliance and the other to the water pipe.

Appliance Problems

Many entire books could be written just on appliance problems. One washer or refrigerator is so complicated that discussing complete repair would take weeks. Still, there are ways to avoid paying a great deal of money for very little work.

The main thing with appliance repair is to verify that you actually have a problem before you call the repairman or take it into the shop. Many times a small, temporary thing will cause indications of a major difficulty and unscrupulous repairmen will charge more than the job is worth. When the appliance begins to malfunction, or when it stops, evaluate what is happening carefully before getting help.

First, did the plug come loose from the wall? It sounds ridiculous, but many people still pay for so-called "repairs" when appliances have simply come unplugged.

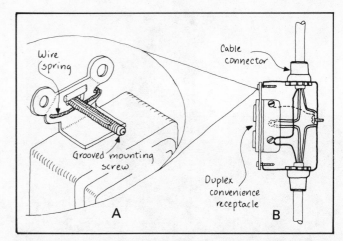

Receptacle grounding detail indicates two methods of providing adequate electrical bonding of the switch or outlet receptacle to the electrical box to maintain grounding continuity. In sketch (A), a built-in wire spring is provided in some devices so proper box contact is made when the device is screwed to the box. In sketch (B), an alternative method. The dashed line which represents a bonding jumper wire from the bonding screw terminal to the box ground screw. The National Electrical Code requires bonding of all electrical system enclosures such as raceways, cable armor, cable sheath, frames, fittings, and other noncurrent-carrying metal parts.

Second, and this is especially true of washers and dryers, look to see that the reset button (wherever it is hidden) has not been tripped. Most larger appliances have their own circuit breakers, called "reset buttons," somewhere in the back or underneath. A temporary load condition (i.e., too many clothes in a dryer) can trip this breaker.

First the plug, then the reset button. If they are both working properly, go back and check the circuit breaker or fuse in the house circuitry.

Assume for as long as possible that the appliance is actually all right and that there is something else causing the problem.

Finally, when you are certain it isn't merely a circuit breaker or the plug has not come loose from the wall, check where the power line is connected to the appliance. Often moving an appliance will work the cord loose and you might find it simply a matter of tightening a screw or replugging a loose plug.

In the end, if the appliance is bad, try the manufacturer before you call the repairman. Even if the appliance is old, even if you do not think it is a defect, drop a note to them and explain that it broke down and ask them to fix it. It will surprise you how often they actually will either fix it or at least absorb part of the cost of labor and/or material.

Heating Systems

Types of Systems

Brief descriptions are given here for heating systems available which conform to generalized repair methods.

Forced Air Systems The most common system: air is heated—usually in a flame chamber or by electrical methods—and then blown through ducting throughout the house.

Hot-Water Heating Second most common, in the system the water is heated and run through the house in piping, with a radiator unit in each room.

Electrical Baseboard Heating In each room an electrical heating unit along the baseboard—usually a straight radiator with hot wires or a water filled unit heated by electrical wires—is controlled by a thermostat.

Radiation Ceiling Units Electrical wires embedded in the drywall in the ceiling—are made warm by current. The wires radiate heat down into the room.

Steam Radiation Units A boiler in the basement heats steam and the steam is circulated through the house through piping, with radiators in each room. Very old houses use this method, which is usually cranky.

Maintenance

As might be expected, and as covered briefly in the first chapter, the best method of heating system "repair" is a good maintenance system. Keep it clean and running right and you probably won't have to worry about specific repairs.

To that end, listed below are some maintenance considerations which can help a great deal (they will be followed by specific repair procedures for breakdown situations).

Keep the filters fresh. This is for forced air systems, obviously, but clean filters allow a much easier air flow and more heat for less money.

Actual replacement of filters is simply a matter of removing the access panel on the side of the heater and sliding the air filter out. Just throw it away and

TROUBLE-SHOOTING CHART
HEATING SYSTEMS

Symptoms	Thermostat (wires soldered in thermostat?)	Lack of energy source	Heater breaker check	Main house breaker check	Change filters	Dust on grates	Lint in grates	Calling about general power outage	Opening in duct to room	Jammed duct stop (grate cover)	Obstruction of grate (box or drape)	Oil blower bearing	Oil pump bearing	Fitting on heater element or radiator
No heat to house	X	X	X	X				X						
No heat to room	X		X					X		X	X	X		
Low heat to house	X	X			X	X	X	X				X		
Low heat to room	X				X	X	X		X	X	X			
Strange "labored" sound from heating system					X				X			X	X	
Dampness on wall/floor														X
Slight chill; shoulder chill	X				X	X	X	X	X	X				
Dust from forced air duct					X				X					
Noticeable high humidity														X
Breaker won't hold on blower motor					X				X			X		
High-pitched squeal from heating system					X							X	X	

replace it with one of the correct size.

Keep the floor grates clean of lint—use the vacuum cleaner to insure easy movement of air.

Wrap the heater ducts in the basement with insulation; just wrap and tape if they are exposed. The heat loss from bare ducts is enormous.

Make sure all joints in ducting are taped with duct tape and are airtight. While doing this you might check around basement windows and use the tape to make a tight air seal and to keep cold air from being "sucked" into the basement by the heater system.

Oil the bearings on the blower fan. Or, if you have a hot-water heating system, oil the bearings on the pump motor. Pump bearings are inside the pump motor on the hot-water heating system (on the side of the boiler assembly). On the motor there will be a small oil-cap filler area. Lift the little spring-lid device and squirt a touch of oil in the hole.

For hot-water systems, use a vacuum cleaner to take all dust off all the baseboard units. Take the covers off and vacuum down in the pipes and fins. Dust greatly affects the heat-transfer qualities of the fin system.

Check the entire hot-water system for seep-leaks, especially on the hot water side of the piping, where it goes up to the actual heating elements. Leaks can be fixed by draining the system and soldering as previously covered, but if allowed to continue they will lose more heat than you think. Drops add up fast.

Electric heating cable is usually located in the ceiling. Drawing courtesy of Dept. of Agriculture

Soap-check all exposed gas connections, whether you have a hot-water system or forced air. Use soap bubbles to check all joints to make sure there are no leaks. (Gas leaks will make obvious bubbles in the soap.) To repair, tighten the fitting with a wrench.

Vacuum the outside of the heater whether it is forced air or hot water. Dust will get into bearings, blowers, fittings and flame jets. If kept clean, there will be less trouble down the line.

Specific-Trouble Repairs

As previously stated, there are so many different kinds of systems that going into detail on any one could take volumes. There are, however, basic repair methods that apply to all.

As with many other forms of household repairs, the most dangerous thing you can do is to jump to expensive conclusions. Then, too, there are many shady operators dealing in the whole area of heating systems that it is best to exhaust all possibilities before calling the contractor. Do not assume anything, and only call in professional help when you're absolutely sure you cannot fix it yourself. The truth is that most heating systems are very simple and well-made, and genuinely break down only rarely.

If the heat just stops, which is the most common symptom, don't reach for the phone. First go down in the basement or wherever the heater is located and visually study it. Don't just look at it, but listen to it as well.

Most often the energy supply has stopped. If you have a gas input, check to make certain the gas is still coming to the heater, and that there is flame in the flame compartment. If you are on electricity, ascertain that the breakers have not tripped and cut off the energy. Really get in there and look.

If there is flame or heat energy evident, check the distribution system. It could be that a blower or pump has tripped a "reset" switch which is quite common. If so, reset the switch by pushing it in and holding it for a moment and then wait to see if everything kicks on and works properly. Line surge or temporary overload could trigger the breaker, which might be more sensitive than the regular house breakers, and the trouble may not occur again for years.

If there is flame or heat energy, and no breaker is tripped, check back at the regular house breakers. If they have not been tripped, then the trouble may be approaching a point where it is necessary to call in a contractor.

The main thing is to approach the system with logic. When there is no heat to the house, look to the source of the heat. If there is fire or energy in the flame chamber, check the distribution. If there is no

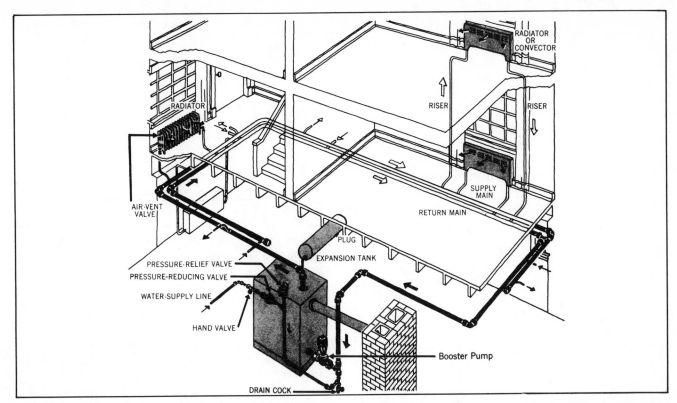

Two-pipe forced hot-water system has one pipe supplying hot water to the room-heating units while the other pipe returns cooled water to the boiler. Drawing courtesy of Dept. of Agriculture

evident problem there (a visually burned-out motor, a switch knocked accidentally off), then recheck.

Relighting Pilot Lights (gas or propane)

First and most important, find the written instructions on the heater in the vicinity of the pilot. Keep looking until you find them. If there are no instructions, a general method follows:

- Turn the gas control knob to the "pilot" position
- Light a match or twisted piece of paper and hold it at the little nozzle where the pilot light burns (easily seen)
- Depress the pilot light "push-button" near the gas control knob and note that pilot light ignites—hold button down for a full minute or more until pilot light stays ignited when push-button is released
- Turn gas control knob to "on" or "heat" position and note that heater comes on

Only call in a heating contractor when you have completely exhausted your own abilities to study the systems involved. Then do so only with utmost caution, and watch the repairman while he works on the heater.

If you are in a fairly new home (ten years or less) check for a home manual for the type of heating system. If there is one available, read it thoroughly. If you are just buying a home, it is a good idea to get addresses from equipment tags on various and sundry appliances and write away for the manual for each item. It can mean a difference of hundreds

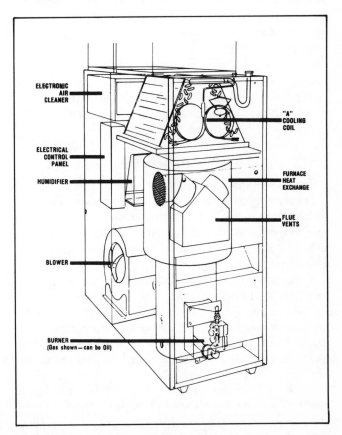

Modern forced warm-air furnaces are very popular; this one heats with gas. Drawing courtesy of Dept. of Agriculture

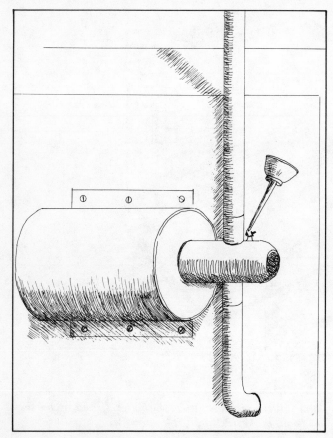

All you need are two or three squirts of oil into the bearing of the pump motor.

of dollars, literally, in future home repair bills. Many of the manuals even include problem-solving breakdown charts which greatly simplify repair work and practically nullify the need for calling in a contractor.

Fireplaces

Smoke Backup When a chimney fails to draw properly for no known obvious reason, it does not necessarily mean you have a serious problem. Usually the reason for smoke backup is that the chimney is cold and is sending cold air falling back down, carrying smoke with it.

First, get some ventilation in the room so there's no chance of suffocation.

Twist a newspaper, light the end and, before lighting a normal fire in the fireplace or heating unit, allow the flames from the newspaper to go up the chimney, establishing an upward movement of hot air.

This will almost always stop smoke backup. If not, call a chimney-cleaning company to unclog the flue.

Method of Sealing Joints A method of closing uncemented flue joints without tearing out the chimney has been used with success in some instan-

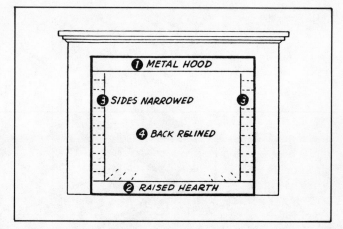

The flue area should not be less than the area of the fireplace opening. Where too small to carry off products of combustion, remedy may be found in reducing the size of the opening. Some corrective measures (1) install a shallow hood of metal beneath the fireplace breast. This also helps in cases where the damper position is too low. (2) Other ways of reducing the opening are to raise the hearth by laying one or two courses of brick over the old hearth. (3) Where drastic reduction is needed narrow the sides of the opening or (4) reline the back.

ces. It involves the use of a traveling plug and fairly thin grout. As a plug, a canvas bag is sometimes employed, stuffed with rags or papers and weighted with bricks in the bottom. When lowered into a flue from the top, by means of a line or pole, it should fit fairly tight, but not too tight to restrict motion. The method to use is to stop it just below the level of each flue joint and pour grout down the flue. When stopped by the plug, the grout flows into the open joint. After the joint appears filled, the plug may be lifted and lowered a few times, producing a swabbing effect. Then it is lowered to the succeeding joint and the operation repeated.

Ashpit Clogged Difficulty sometimes encountered in removing ashes from ashpits may be handled by making pits with uniform sectional areas and smoothing walls. When pits or chutes are offset in passing a fireplace on a lower floor, all possible care must be taken to avoid roughness or sharp changes of direction. Wall leakage, particularly in the basement wall, permits water to seep in and convert ashes into a soaked and tightly packed mass. More difficult conditions may call for tearing out masonry and treating obstructions.

Paints and Finishes

Broadly speaking, dealing with paints and finishes becomes a matter of bracketing the finishes in categories.

Either it is an exterior covering or an interior one; either it is a water base or an oil base finish; either it is enamel or latex (acrylic) based paint.

Repair of your particular finish depends on the bracket it falls into, and that means you must first identify the kind of finish. Putting an interior plastic-based paint on an exterior, enamel base paint will not do anything but cause further and more difficult problems.

Before doing any kind of repair on any kind of painted or finished surface, know the paint you are dealing with. If in doubt, take a chip or sample to the paint store and have it identified.

Exteriors

There was a time when all exterior painting was enamel because it was the only type strong enough to withstand the weather and sun. Now they have perfectly acceptable exterior plastic-based paints that even look like enamel, and for that reason identifying them is sometimes difficult. Again, take a chip to a paint store for positive identification, and be sure to take the chip from the immediate area of the repair place.

Chips or Peeling As for actual repair work on exterior paint, you need a wire brush, a small throwaway paint brush and a small can of the right colored paint (matched from the chip). This of course is for small areas, for common repair of a damaged surface. For whole repainting of the outside of a house the work is extensive, and should be considered remodeling rather than repair. But for the small repair, the work is simple: use the wire brush to thoroughly "scrub" the area to be touched up or repainted. Extend this scrubbing not just to the limits of the damage but out into the good paint around it as well. This will clean the surface and make it slightly abrasive so it will take the paint more tightly. Scrub very hard, and wipe with a dry rag. Then paint in coats. Allow the first one to dry well and stand back ten or fifteen feet to see how it blends in when dry. If it needs to be darker, try another coat. If it does not seem right after the second coat has dried completely, you have a paint mismatch. Either live with it, or take another chip

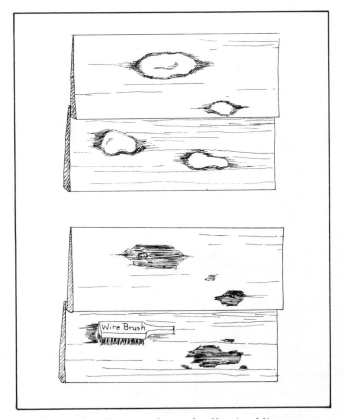

Use a wire brush to gently work off paint blisters.

down to the paint store for a second try at the right color. (This happens, occasionally especially with red-based colors; they are difficult to match.)

Blistering Blistering of exterior paint is probably the most common paint repair. If it simply pocks here and there, repair by scrubbing and perhaps sanding lightly, then repaint in spots as per above. Be sure the blisters are not only broken off but that the surrounding surfaces are well taken down, clean, and unflaked.

If blisters are extensive and cover whole sections of wall, repair is likewise extensive and more physically oriented. The wall must be scraped, *each* blister scrubbed and sanded, then the whole wall painted It is a lot of work and some of it requires working on a ladder.

Fading Fading of exterior surfaces is another common finish problem. Unfortunately the only true repair is to repaint the whole thing. But before you start measuring the square feet to buy gallons of paint, be certain the wall *is* faded. Quite often a

EXTERIOR PAINT AND OTHER FINISHES

Surface Types	Oil or oil-alkyd paint	Cement powder paint	Exterior clear finish	Aluminum paint	Wood stain	Roof coating	Trim paint	Porch & deck paint	Primer or undercoater	Metal primer	Latex house paint	Water repellent
Wood Surfaces Clapboard	X.			X					X		X.	
Natural Wood Siding and Trim			X		X							
Shutters and other trim	X.						X.		X		X.	
Wood Frame Windows	X.			X			X.		X		X.	
Wood Porch Floor								X				
Wood Shingle Roof					X							X
Metal Surfaces Aluminum Windows	X.			X			X.			X	X.	
Steel Windows	X.			X.			X.			X	X.	
Metal Roof	X.									X	X.	
Metal Siding	X.			X.			X.			X	X.	
Copper Surfaces			X									
Galvanized Surfaces	X.			X.			X.			X	X.	
Iron Surfaces	X.			X.			X.			X	X.	
Miscellaneous Asbestos Cement	X.								X		. X	
Brick	X.	X		X					X		X	
Cement and Cinder Block	X.	X		X					X		X	
Concrete/Masonry Porches and Floors								X			X	
Coal Tar Felt Roof						X						
Stucco	X.	X		X					X		X	

· dot at right of X indicates a primer or sealer may be needed before finishing coat is applied
SOURCE: U.S. Department of Commerce

Large blisters formed and broke under this eave. Cause was moisture reaching the crawl space above the eave, below the sloping roof.

An open invitation to trouble is improper coating application. Blisters will probably form because an oil paint is being applied over condensed moisture, thereby lessening adhesive forces.

Incompatible topcoat flaked off this wood after a few months. Primer and topcoat came from different manufacturers.

thin patina of silt-dust (usual if you live near a dirt road) will give the impression of fading. Try hosing the house down, then let it dry well. It is worth a try and the "fading" might just disappear.

If you live in a smoggy area, the atmosphere can make the finish look faded. Debris collects in the cracks and on the flat surfaces. Try warm-to-hot water with a mild detergent and a soft brush or rag; quite often the wash will restore the finish without repainting.

Redwood and Cedar Redwood and cedar do not require a finish, and are usually just allowed to age. Now and then you will find it has been oiled. If the oil has faded or "sunk" into the wood, repair is simple. Just get some prepared linseed oil and treat the wood to another coat, applying with a brush. Make sure the surface is clean, of course; dust with a broom before applying the oil.

Sometimes the redwood or cedar shake exterior requiring repair will have been bleached. The bleach hastens redwood's natural color change and produces a permanent driftwood gray. One or two coats applied with roller or brush to your repaired section will help match the new redwood to the old.

WOOD CLASSIFICATION ACCORDING TO OPENNESS OF PORES				
Alder	X			X	Stains well
Ash		X	X		Needs filler
Aspen		X		X	Paints well
Basswood		X		X	Paints well
Beech		X		X	Varnishes well, paints poorly
Birch		X		X	Paints and varnishes well
Cedar	X			X	Paints and varnishes well
Cherry		X		X	Varnishes well
Chestnut		X	X		Requires filler, paints poorly
Cottonwood		X		X	Paints well
Cypress		X		X	Paints and varnishes well
Elm		X	X		Requires filler, paints poorly
Fir	X			X	Paints poorly
Gum		X		X	Varnishes well
Hemlock	X			X	Paints fairly well
Hickory		X	X		Needs filler
Mahogany		X	X		Needs filler
Maple		X		X	Varnishes well
Oak		X	X		Needs filler
Pine	X			X	Variable
Teak		X	X		Needs filler
Walnut		X	X		Needs filler
Redwood	X				Paints well
	Soft Wood	Hard Wood	Open Pore	Closed Pore	Notes

A sharp scraper from your paint or hardware store combined with a little muscle can reduce blisters and flaking surfaces almost level. Sandpaper finishes the leveling process.

This is a special flat brush with bristles arranged to paint under siding.

Other possible finishes to be found on your redwood or shake exterior are stains, either light- or heavy-bodied. They do not obscure the grain. Two coats are required.

If no other finish is applied, a water repellent is a good idea. The use of a water repellent will enable you to later change to any other finish without additional preparation. Cuprinol #20, Woodlife, or Pentaseal will all do an adequate job.

If for some reason the wood has been painted, be sure that the paint you choose not only matches the original color but is specifically intended for use on exterior redwood. One prime and two finish coats are recommended, and it is a good practice to be wary of the sun when painting. Try not to let the

sun's rays strike the surface during or immediately after painting.

Plywood New plywood used for your repair should be given a quick edge-sealing of all panels before installation. This will minimize moisture damage and size variation due to rising and falling humidity.

If panels are not to be painted, such as textured plywood finished with stain, apply a liberal application of water repellent preservative compatible with any finish to be applied later. Horizontal edges, particularly lower drip edges of siding, should be treated. If you want to mask all characteristics other than texture, use an oil, latex emulsion opaque, or highly pigmented stain.

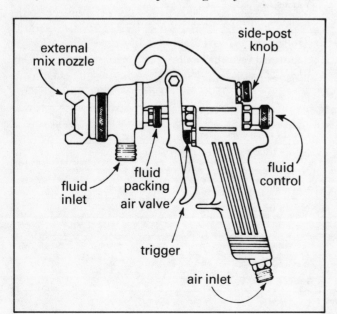

Spray gun

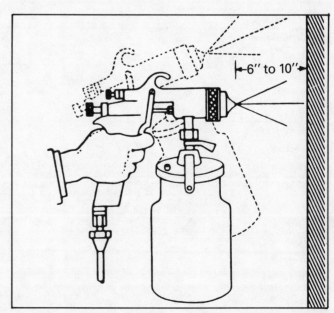

Positioning of a spray gun

If paint will be used, use a primer and two coats. The best time to paint is during dry, clear weather above 50°F. and below 95°F.

Interiors

Again, the most important requirement for interior repairs is knowledge of the kind of finish being repaired. Take a chip to the local paint outlet. After determining the kind of finish, evaluate the damage.

Blistering With interiors as well as exteriors, a primary problem is blistering—especially in humid rooms (bathrooms) or where heat might be a factor (the kitchen or over the heating stove). In these cases, a fan will prevent future blistering.

The repair is the same as for exterior work. "Pop" the blister, scrub it and the surrounding area with a wire brush to insure that it is clean, and match the color by taking a chip from right next to the damaged area. Paint, again, in coats. Allow the first coat to dry well, see how it matches, then add another.

Fading Fading is, oddly, more of a problem inside the house than outside. The sun will work through a window and leave a very definite color line where it cooks the finish out of the paint. The obvious repair, naturally, is to just repaint the affected wall after making certain that it is not just dirt. Try washing with warm water and mild detergent. But if the faded area is small, say down in the corner of the wall, you might try treating it as a simple small repair. Match the paint by taking a chip from the good area and paint by "feathering" the new paint job into the old. Do it a coat at a time, and let dry well before deciding whether or not you have a good color match.

Yellowing Yellowing is another problem that seems to happen more indoors than out, usually with off-white colors. The repair is to repaint, but first try washing the wall or ceiling with warm water and detergent. It might remove some of the paint if the original painters did not do a proper job, but that is no great loss since you would have to repaint anyway. If the yellowing does not wash off, clean well and repaint to match.

Some general things to remember on interior painting: first, make *certain* everything is clean, dry and free of dust; dirt, grease or oil will just negate the whole repair because the new paint will lift off as soon as it has dried. Second, match not just the color, but the application method as well. If the original finish was applied with a brush, then do the repair with a brush. If the original job was done with a roller, then you do the same—although you can use the small roller to cut expenses. Also, match the direction of application as well as method. If the brush strokes were originally vertical, sweeping sideways will stand out like a sore thumb.

Take your time and do the job properly the first time and there is a chance you will not have to repair your repair later. Hand in hand with doing the job right is the understanding of how paints should be used, and the proper application for the proper use.

Do not try shortcuts that will simply bounce back on you later and cause an even bigger headache. Trying to use an interior latex base paint for outside purposes to save a dollar just will not work. The same goes for using a very cheap, plastic base paint in a humid area like in a shower stall or over the humidifier. The paint will just bubble off inside a month or so and you will have to do it over.

Painting, more than any other house repair, will not tolerate shortcuts.

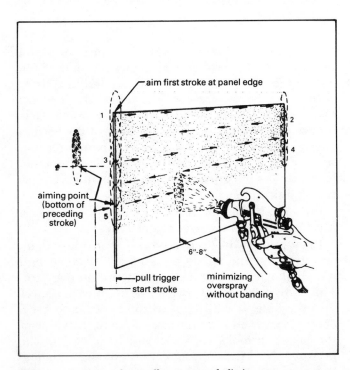

When spraying a large flat area a definite pattern must be followed by the painter if good results are to be achieved. Note also that there is an optimal distance from the spray gun orifice to the work surface.

Siding Repairs

From a purely numerical standpoint there are so many kinds of siding, from aluminum to wood to masonite to plastic—and so many things can go wrong with all of them.

Still, here are some general repair tips that can save a great deal of time and money, plus notes on several of the more popularly used forms of siding.

Before doing repair on any kind of siding it is good to consider why you need the repair. One good reason is that prompt repair can prevent further deterioration, rust, and later expense. Another reason is the rapid climb in home value, and the fact that buyers often base their offers on what they see when they first come upon a house. You might lose or make several thousand dollars when/if you sell your home merely because of the condition of the siding.

So no matter the kind of siding or the nature of the repair, the quality of work can vastly affect the amount of money you ultimately get for your home. This means you must take your time and do a good job.

Wood Siding

Using wood for siding—whether it be plywood, shingle, or lap siding—is becoming more expensive. The material is common on older homes but some experts predict that in not too many years wood siding will be virtually nonexistent because of its cost. For this reason, special care should be taken in repair.

Actually, the damage siding can sustain and still be repaired is limited to that caused by weather and by accident.

If the wood is raw cedar or redwood the weather will not hurt it, and the only repair necessary is replacement of the damaged piece.

If the siding is painted, see the chapter on "Finishes" for correct paints and application methods, remembering of course to match faded colors correctly.

Lap Siding Cracks are the most common damage found in lap siding, other than paint fading. Usually a whole long piece cracks and falls away, calling for replacement of a whole board of siding.

Replacement is not as hard as you might think. Using a small crowbar and claw hammer "raise" the siding board, gently, directly above the board to be replaced and prop it up with scraps of wood.

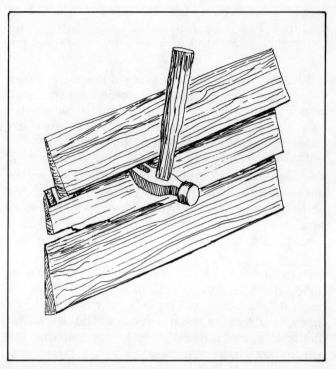

Remember that lap-siding is vulnerable to dents. Be careful when working with it.

Now tear out the damaged piece of siding and replace it with a new matching piece from the lumberyard. Nail the new board into underlying studs with 2d or 3d galvanized box nails. Don't worry about studs if underlying sheathing is wood. It is best to nail siding above the top edge of the bottom boards; this permits the siding to expand and contract. Set the bottom nails slightly with a punch, then nail the old top board back down and set those nails slightly too.

Either paint to match, or let the weather work on it if the wood is raw redwood or cedar.

Plywood Siding (raw wood) For major damage, tear out the whole piece of old plywood and match it with a new piece from the lumberyard. Then nail it up. Do not try to piece in a part of a sheet into the hole. It will be nearly impossible to get a decent match and the damage done to the value of the house in looks will far exceed the cost of the plywood. Nail the siding, as in all outside applications, using galvanized nails with heads to avoid rust and warpage.

"Lifting" Dents In both lap siding and plywood, raw or painted, you can repair one kind of

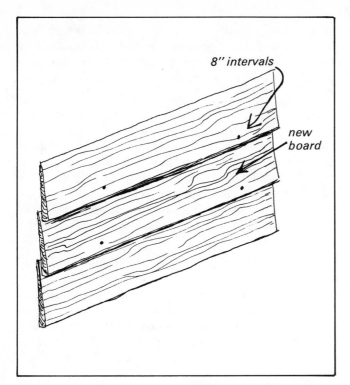

Raise the old siding piece; slip in the new matching board. Nail through the old siding board into the top edge of the new piece, and through the new board into the top of the board below.

Using a punch, lightly tap the nails just under the surface. Then color with a stain or color stick.

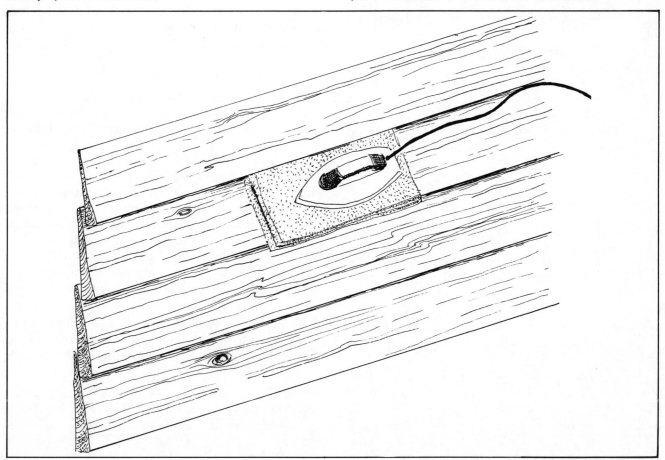

Just have the rag damp, and the iron very hot, and watch carefully to stop as soon as the dent is lifted.

ding without jerking the whole board or panel off the wall.

When a small dent occurs—a compression dent and not a tear or gouge, the way a mower might dent when it hits the wall, or a car moving just part of that last inch before stopping—try taking an old damp towel to "iron" the dent out. Just place one thickness of the damp towel over the dent and use your iron, set very hot, to steam the wood back out to its original level; press the iron down hard on the towel so the steam works well into the dent. Quite often this will pull the dent back so that it is difficult to see the damaged place.

Be sure to use a grounded, three-wire extension cord when you take the iron outside.

Shingle Siding The usual problem with shingle or shake siding is a split piece falling out either as a result of age or some blow; and the repair is to replace the piece that has fallen out.

Buy a small packet of shingles or shakes from the lumberyard and split a piece with a butcher knife or hatchet until it fits the hole.

Then carefully "raise" the shingles above the damaged one and slide the tail or thin portion up under the shingles. Nail as high as possible with galvanized nails (8d or 10d). Do not worry that the shingle seems to stand out. It will quickly weather in.

Usually the full shingle will not fit completely under the row above, but will hit a nail before the bottom or butt of the shingle comes up far enough to align properly with the butts of the shingles already on the wall. Simply cut enough off the thin end to allow the edge to come up to the right place before nailing. It will not leak or look unprofessional.

Metal Siding

As might be expected, the only repair possible with damaged metal siding is complete replacement of the damaged section. Metal siding cannot be steamed smooth or even popped back out the way a body worker repairs the fender on a car.

Replacement methods vary drastically, depending on the kind of metal siding you have and the company who makes it. Complete, specific instructions as to repair and replacement should come with the material when you buy it.

Wear a cheap pair of leather gloves. All metal siding seems to be made of old knives, and small cuts and nicks are the rule.

Remember that all metal, even sheet steel or galvanized steel, has absolutely *zero* resiliency. A hammer dent in wood siding barely shows and can be

steamed out easily with your iron. A hammer dent in aluminum siding shows terribly and cannot be fixed properly without replacement, so be extremely careful when you are putting the new material on.

Pull off the damaged piece, being careful not to damage those which are still on the wall. You will note that it was nailed along the top edge, and that the replacement piece likewise has a strip along the top edge for nailing. First, after measuring against the old piece, use some very good tinsnips or very poor scissors to cut the new piece of siding. Then work the piece in place, up beneath the top piece with the nailer strip agianst the wall, and over the bottom piece.

Then, awkwardly prying the top piece up, nail with 8d galvanized nails along the strip, up-under, being careful not to miss and to dent the siding. A nail every foot or so will do, and when you are finished nailing just allow the siding to hang down. If it sticks out warp it into place with your hands, until it pushes in with the spring of the metal.

Plastic Siding

Plastic siding, either in lap-wood form or simulated plywood sheets, is much like metal in that severe damage demands replacement of the entire piece if it is to look good. Even then colors rarely seem to match because the sun fades the old siding and the new color seems too rich. Often you must paint over it all to overcome this.

On small dents or dings, a great deal of success has been made by filling the damaged spot with premixed fiberglass putty they sell for boat repair. It is necessary to mix it with a catalyst, as per instructions on the can. It hardens fast, but can be tapped and textured with your finger to match the simulated wood grain common with vinyl siding, or it can be sanded smooth to match a smooth surface. Once set it is a simple matter to take a small sample of paint to the local paint store, match it to their chips and touch up the damaged area so that it is almost impossible to tell where the problem was, and it is much cheaper than buying a whole new piece.

Be sure to wear throwaway rubber gloves when working with the putty, and a respirator mask if you intend doing any extensive sanding. The glass fibers are dangerous to breathe.

This fiberglass putty method was tried on the metal siding also, but it did not work well. It adhered at first and seemed adequate for small repair jobs, but over any length of time it came loose and looked cheaply done.

Hand tools for siding application, are suggested in the Installation Manual for applications of Alcoa Building Products. Practices and tools used by siding specialists may vary from one area to another. The tools shown are identified as follows: (1) chalk line reel, (2) folding rule, (3) 2 or 4 foot level, (4) carpenter's steel square, (5) caulking gun, (6) electric saw with aluminum cutting blade, (7) claw hammer, (8) double-action aviation snips, (9) utility knife, (10) metal file, (11) fine-toothed hacksaw, (12) tinsnips, (13) conventional cross-cut handsaw, (14) nail set.

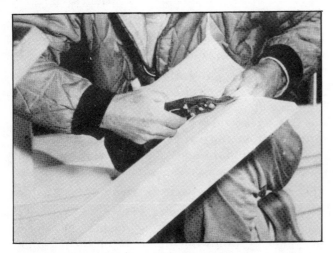

Cut and crimp tools for use with vinyl siding include the precision aviation-type curved-blade snips whose double-acting blades easily follow cutting marks in vinyl and a pliers-like hand tool called a "Snap-lock Punch." It makes a depression crimp in vinyl cut edges that allow the edge to be inserted into trim strips and locked into position.

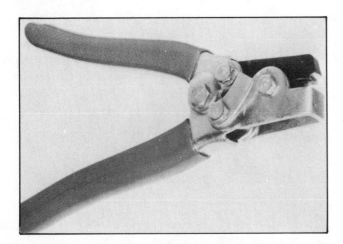

Fiberboard Siding

Made of pressed board to simulate lap-wood siding or plywood rough-sawn sheets, repair requires replacement of the whole piece if damage is relatively severe.

Dings, gouges and dents can be fixed with fiberglass putty, being careful to match any simulated

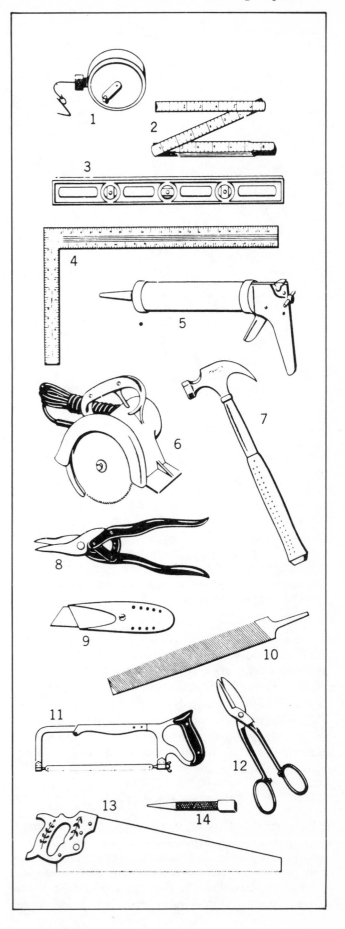

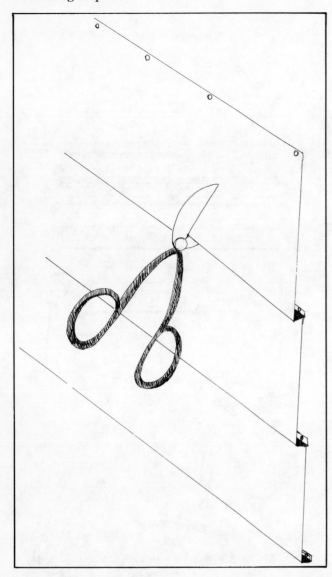

Tinsips work best on metal siding. Be careful not to dent or bend the new siding piece.

your fingers, using a patting motion to "suck" out the cement in little puckers.

Over a large area the work has to be done in two stages. First, after cleaning out all loose and broken particles, use a flat, float-trowel to plaster the entire area smoothly, and bring it out so that it is even with the surrounding wall. Again, use the premix to avoid confusion. Make a thick mixture, adding water slowly as you mix it in a bucket until the cement is about the consistency of loose bread dough—so it will hold a ball if formed in your hand.

Put it on with wide sweeps, and work it well into the mesh-backing already there, "feathering" the patch-mud into the old.

Then let it dry overnight. When it has had a chance to become hard but is still damp—the next day—mix up a batch of fairly runny cement, about like thin cream of wheat. This you apply with a patting motion and an old, coarse sponge. It is easy, and you will find the stucco easy to match after a bit of practice.

Let the patch cure well for several days before painting to match.

For smooth-textured patching you mix the cement the same way, following directions on the package. Stop once the smooth patch has been well feathered

wood grain. If the grain does not match the first time, or it does not look pleasing for some reason, you can easily use a screwdriver or chisel to "pop" out the repair job and do it over.

Paint to match when dry and the repair is finished.

Be certain, even with metal or plastic siding, that on *any* outside application you are using galvanized nails. Anything else will rust and not only look awful but let the job down.

Cement Siding

Stucco In repairing stucco a great deal depends on the size of the damaged area. For small spots, pull out all the old, dry, and loose stucco around the hole and patch with a handful of thick masonry mortar. Premixed works fine and saves the trouble of mixing sand with cement. Texture to match with

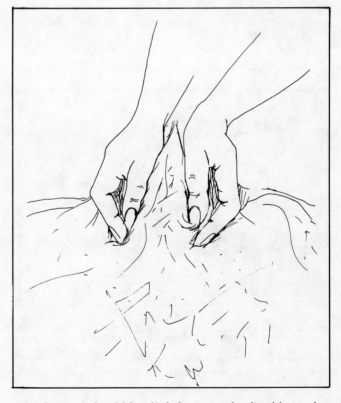

Adobe mud should be slightly runny for final layer, but the base mud should hold a peak when pushed with palm.

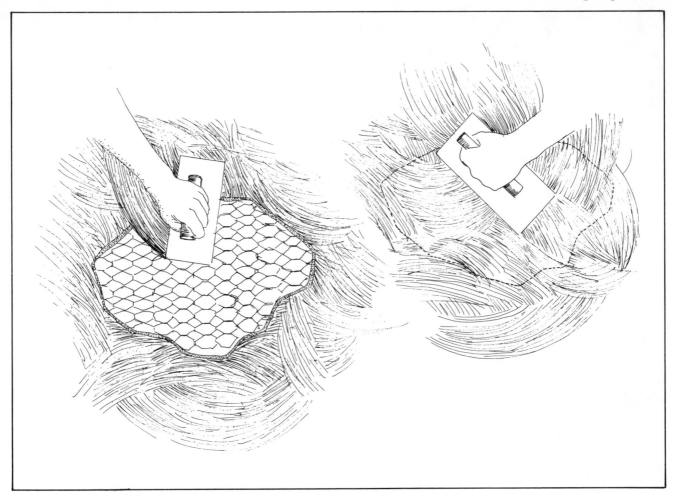

Use a float trowel to plaster smoothly. Then "feather" the new patch mud into the old.

in. In patching deep holes in concrete walls (for example, on the back of a garage when a car has given it a heavy whack), be sure the hole to be patched is well cleaned and brushed out to insure a good bond. It often helps to dampen the hole before patching because water strengthens cement.

Paint using a good concrete paint. Taking short-cuts with cement is usually fruitless; the paint will just lift off later.

Adobe Adobe mud patching is in a class by itself, but easy and even fun to do.

To patch adobe, first clean the damaged area thoroughly, and let dry. Then mix up some adobe mud, with a touch of cement (about 20 to 1) if you like, from the same area as the original bricks—so the earth-color will match and apply with your hand or a flat trowel.

To mix adobe base mud, use "tight" earth and add water until mud holds a slight peak when pushed together with your palms. Use this for plastering.

Do not overdo it. If the patch job is deep, apply it in several layers, with the mud again like cream of wheat, to avoid excessive cracking. It is not necessary to mix straw into the plastering mud of adobe; it makes the mud lumpy, difficult to smear well, and hard to work smooth.

For bricks mix up a slightly more runny compound; add straw by the large handful—one for each molded brick. Let bricks cure several days in the sun before using them.

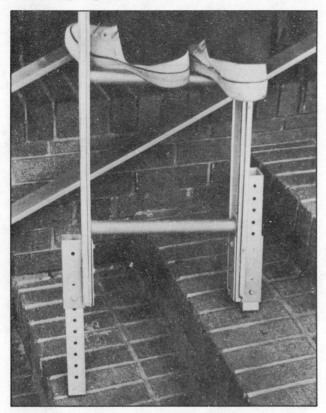

On uneven ground use ladders with extension legs like the model shown above in use on brick steps. The extension legs have nonskid feet and are adjustable to 9 inches in ¼-inch increments. Photo courtesy of Alproco, Inc.

The U-shaped aluminum arm at the top of the extension ladder in above photo is called the "Saf-T-Arm" because it holds the ladder away from the vertical surface, allowing ample working room. No bending backward necessary. An inexpensive device that bolts on most ladders. Photo courtesy of Fracon Company, Inc.

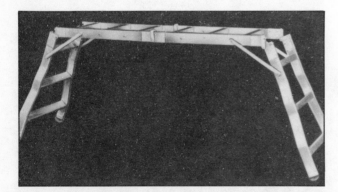

Aluminum scaffold devices of use in residing work include the multiposition folding ladder (above). It can be used in inverted-U form as a low scaffold or in inverted-V form like a stepladder. Photo courtesy of Goldblatt Tool Co.

The aluminum scaffold planks (right) are able to do double-duty as ladders. The metal devices on which they rest are foot-operated jacks that the workman on the scaffold can raise or lower without stepping off the scaffold. They ride up and down a pair of 2x6 posts held in vertical position by roof plates. Photo courtesy of R. D. Werner Co.

Roof Repair

Basically, damage to a roof that requires repair comes under one of two categories; it is either dramatic or insidious.

Either your roof is attacked violently by nature, torn apart by wind or hail, or a slow crippling problem will develop that spreads over the entire roof.

In either case repair is mandatory, before a leak can do damage to the interior of the house. Water can wreck drywall the way fire melts wax. Also, in both cases the repair method depends entirely on the material from which the roof is constructed.

Composition Shingle

The most popular, most widely used, and probably least expensive roof is the asphalt or composition shingle roof. For those unfamiliar with roofing materials, this is the type of shingle that seems to be covered with a gritty substance and is made out of a thick tar-papery material.

Within the spectrum of composition shingles, there are two kinds of application methods—the straight shingle and the interlocking shingle. The straight shingle is simply nailed down, with the roofing nails hidden from view by the next row of shingles. The interlocking shingles, which are used in high wind areas, are also nailed down but they have a secondary holding power because two little "tails" on either end lock into the two "tails" on the shingles on either side.

Strangely, of the two forms of damage mentioned it seems easier to successfully repair the catastrophe. The insidious damage results mostly from age deteriorating the shingles themselves, which lends itself less easily to repair.

Insidious Roof Problems As stated, age is the crippler. The sun and weather, over a twenty or thirty year period, truly ruin composition shingles. Leaks begin to show up here and there. Repair is elemental, but again, difficult. Buy a small (1 gal.) can of roofing tar, or mastic, and wear soft-soled shoes so as not to further damage the roof.

Look for the hole somewhere above the leak spot where it comes through the roof (usually quite close but not always) and plug it with a dab of tar—just a dab. As the sun cooks, the tar becomes soft; if you put too much on it will actually run down the roof.

If possible, and with great care, lift the shingle and try to get tar underneath as well as on top; work it into the hole gently. It does not take much to stop the leak, and the tar will keep, so do not overdo.

The problem is that when you get that first leak you will probably start to get a lot more of them, assuming the roof is old. You can, of course, keep plugging the holes with tar as they come, but you might want to consider redoing the whole or portions of the roof in the near future.

Catastrophes The most common sudden damage to composition roofs is from wind: a quick, violent wind will rip out two or three shingles, just enough to leave a bad hole in the roof.

Repair is basic, the damage easily seen and fixed. You just take one of the damaged shingles to the lumberyard; match it; buy a packet of shingles (which are handy to have around anyway, just in case) and some roofing nails, and replace the damaged section.

First, gently remove any of the old shingles still remaining, and pull the old nails. Second, as you work in the new shingles (locking them if they are interlocking) it does not hurt to dab them with roofing tar; again, not a lot, but just enough to seal them

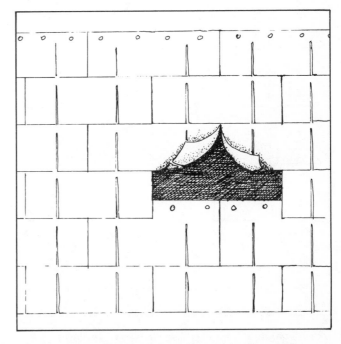

Composition shingles are easily repaired by pulling out the damaged one and nailing in the new; curl up the above shingles to take the new one.

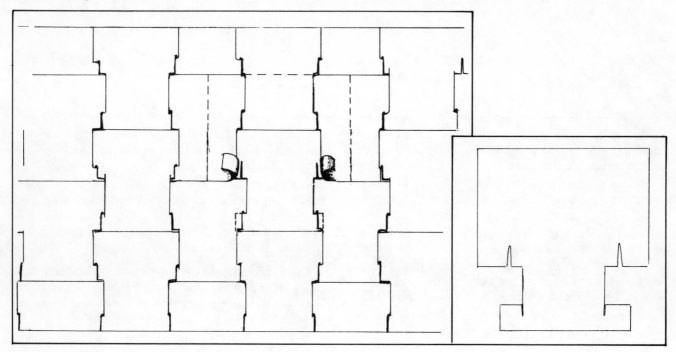

T-lock composition shingles are slightly more complicated. The old shingle comes out, the new one is inserted—but the new shingle has to be interlocked with the old roof. Do this carefully, as the old shingles are often fragile.

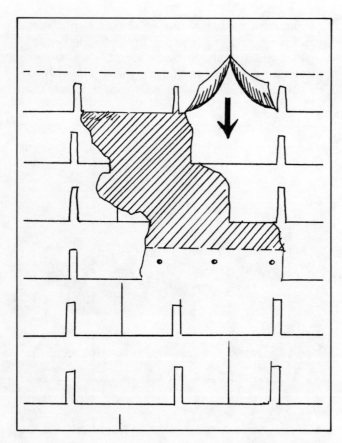

For damage to two or three shingles, leaving a hole, remove old shingles and pull old nails. Work in new shingles, dabbing underside with roofing tar to ensure a good bond.

down. It will insure a good, tight bond and avoid further leaks in the damaged area.

If the damage is massive—if a wind tore off half the roof covering or hail (rarely bad enough to hurt a roof) somehow shredded the entire shingled area, do not try repair on a patch basis. Call your insurance company and recover the whole roof, on a remodeling approach.

Flat Roof—Tar and Gravel

Used on a flat or only slightly pitched roof, the hot-tar-and-gravel surface is probably about the easiest to repair.

Insidious Damage Generally the place where the water shows up inside will be very close to the hole in the roof surface. There is little traveling because the roof is so flat.

Repair is a matter of dabbing some tar or mastic in and around the hole area, then patting some matching gravel or pea rock (from the driveway) into the still-wet tar or mastic. Use a stick to pat the gravel down because the tar is so sticky.

Major Damage The only thing that will wreck a hot-tar-and-gravel roof is probably a hurricane. A new roof put over the old is then about all you can do. Areas or holes up to an inch or so can be patched with the straight-tar-and-gravel method described above.

If a piece a foot or less is ripped out, use tar paper (30# pound felt) and sandwich up the tar and paper,

Footing holds for roof work can be provided by temporarily tacking 2 x 4s in place. Photo above shows new plywood sheathing being applied over old roofing. Footing 2 x 4s are tacked through wood shingle courses, nail holes filled with caulking after removal. Some roofers use sheet metal straps slipped between shingles to hold the footing 2 x 4s.

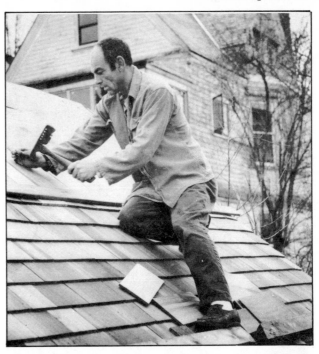

The base upon which new shingles are to be placed needs attention. Nail down or remove protruding roofing nails. Renail split shingles. Replace broken or missing ones. Whether the old roofing is asphalt or wood shingles, get a smooth firm foundation for any new roofing material.

using tar liberally. Cover with matching gravel.

Large holes call for hot patches and/or a new roof. It is not only dangerous because the tar is 600°F., but very difficult.

Wood Shingle—Cedar Shake

Wood shingle and cedar shake roofs are very much a two-edged sword. On the one hand they make a beautiful and durable roof, tight and warm. On the other, wood shingle or cedar shake is probably the most difficult roof material to repair.

Wood roofs are almost always steeply pitched—otherwise the roof will not shed snow and rain sufficiently to keep the shake or shingle from leaking. The pitch angle not only makes working on the roof difficult and hazardous, but leaks tend to "travel" around.

Because of the steepness of the roof the water might be coming through the shingles up near the peak, coming through the tar paper sheathing halfway down and not coming through into the house until it has traveled many feet away from the actual hole.

Insidious Leaks Start, naturally, where the leak is coming through the main roof into the house. If you are lucky the leak will be right there and you can plug it with a tiny bit of tar or mastic or colored (gray) caulking compound. Just a small amount should be squirted into the hole.

Usually your luck is not that good. The leak will be somewhere above the area where it comes through into the house.

The only way to find it is to start a thorough search up the roof using a ladder, taking your time and going inch by inch. Just keep looking, and if you cannot find the hole try again until you do see it. Then plug it with a bit of tar or caulking.

The leak will show itself, either as an open crack or hole or as a missing shingle-piece. You must keep at it until you find the leak. If it is a split-out piece insert a replacement split that is the right width.

1—The first re-roofing strip along eave will be a 5 x 36-inch strip, measured and cut so the 5-inch strip has the black adhesive seal-down stripping near the bottom.

2—Balance of the cut strip can then be further trimmed down 2 inches for another 5-inch wide strip with seal-down adhesive, which can be applied later at the ridges.

3—Then position beginning or starter course of the 5-inch wide strips against butt of the second course of old asphalt shingles, with the seal down stripping near the eave edge.

4—Nail starter strip with four nails per strip, placing the nails at a point just below the seal-down adhesive stripping.

5—Then place second course of single strips trimming the strips down to 10-inch widths. This course is positioned butting to the third course of old shingles.

6—Place third and following courses conventionally, each butting to an old shingle course. This series is from a complete installation set covering Johns-Manville fiberglass shingles.

A pneumatic stapler can save hours of time when doing a re-roofing job. Photo courtesy of Georgia Pacific

Ridge shingles are single-tab widths cut from shingle strips and applied with the same exposure as used with the field shingles. Use one nail on each side of the ridge. With your hands, carefully prebend each ridge shingle. In some areas, suppliers offer precut ridge and hip shingles.

Diagonal application makes for easier shingle handling according to expert roofers; this method is preferred, rather than applying full shingle courses across the roof horizontally.

Major Damage Wind, fire, or hail damage—the three causes of major roof problems with wood surfaces—call for completely replacing the damaged shingles or shakes.

Here the work is simple, although physically demanding. It is much like laying up a small new roof.

Just lay up the shingles or shakes starting at the bottom or eave and work up at the same intervals as the surrounding roof.

When you get to the last row, to facilitate "feeding" the replacement shingles up into the old row above, move across the roof with a claw hammer and loosen the top (next) row of the old undamaged roof, but gently.

Then slide the new shingles up under the old, nail as high as you can, and tap the old row back down on top of the new row.

Of course it is vital to remember the basic principle of all shingle roofing: stagger the shingles so that a whole shingle always covers the crack between two above to avoid leaks.

Also, especially important on steeply pitched roofs but a rule that holds true when working in any high area, take everything slowly and carefully. No roof

Cementing down of new shingles all around the chimney should be done whether old counter-flashing is used or not. If not, then additional cement caulking should be applied along the joint between shingles and the chimney faces.

Sidewall juncture, the point where a roof surface meets the siding of an upper story, also requires the use of a roofing-felt underlayment strip of flashing plus the cementing down of the adjacent shingles.

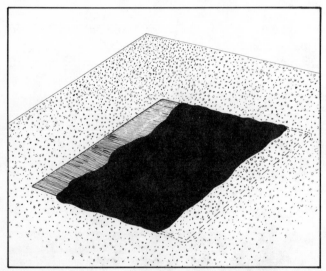

Hot tar and gravel roofs are easily cold-patched. Just remember to wear old clothes and take everything slowly.

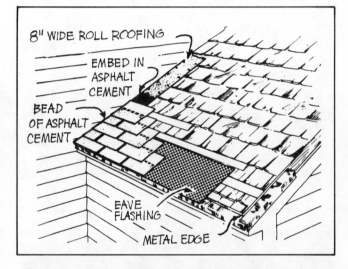

Eave flashing and sidewall flashing with roll roofing cemented down is desirable when new asphalt shingles are being applied over old roofing.

repair is worth a fall and possible severe injury.

On truly steep roofs, as on an A-frame or chalet, repair can be greatly facilitated by renting a set of roof-jacks with which to make a plank-scaffold to stand on. Instructions come with the jacks, but follow directions carefully and exactly.

Special Roofs

There are literally dozens of different specialized roof coverings—from ceramic tube tiles to so-called scientific wonder coverings (generally very risky)—so that we cannot cover each in detail here.

But generally, most of the different roof materials come under the heading of common sense; if you think a repair might work, it probably will work.

Tar, mastic, or closely colored caulking (instructions for use come with caulking, on the tube) will fix most small leaks on any kind of roof.

In cases of metal roofing, where major damage has been sustained, replacement of the whole piece is necessary. Just pry up the "above" section and insert the new piece, caulking everything liberally.

Roll-roofing, which is actually the same as composition or asphalt shingles except that it comes in heavy rolls, take tar well for small jobs. If a large section is damaged, cut out a square and put in light tar paper to fill the hole. Then cut a square of the appropriately colored replacement material purchased from the local lumberyard and nail it in with long roofing nails on about four-inch centers. After nailing, work the tar well into the seams, over the

To repair cedar shakes or shingles, be sure to "roll" them out slightly as in the illustration, so the new shingle goes in easily. Note that the seam between two shingles falls in the central area of the shake below—away from the seam—to avoid leaks.

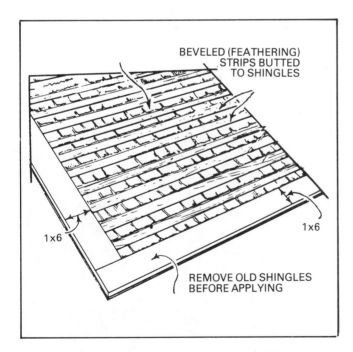

Metal edging applied along eaves and rakes will provide a proper drip edge and prevent moisture backup under the roofing material. Instruction details on these pages and the drawings have been excerpted from the application manual issued by the Asphalt Roofing Manufacturers Association.

Replace shingles on an old wood-shingled roof if there are broken or missing shingles. Simply insert the replacement up under the course above, and nail down.

Add wood strips to firm up the base to which the reroofing materials will be attached. The drawing indicates new six-inch wide strips along eaves and rakes, since these areas are most likely to show decay. Apply strips so top surface is flush with old roofing. At right, feathered strips butt to old wood shingles. Beveled wood siding boards make good feathering strips.

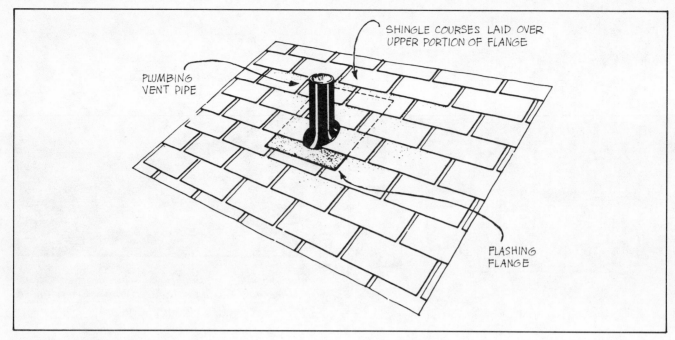

PLUMBING
VENT PIPE

SHINGLE COURSES LAID OVER
UPPER PORTION OF FLANGE

FLASHING
FLANGE

Check flashings at all plumbing stack and vent projections through the roof. Flashing flanges should be interleaved as indicated with the new shingling. If old roofing remains in place, so does the flashing, and the new shingles are cut to fit the projection and cemented down around it.

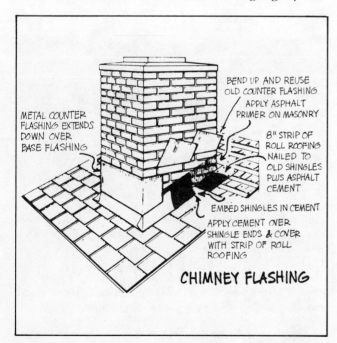

METAL COUNTER
FLASHING EXTENDS
DOWN OVER
BASE FLASHING

BEND UP AND REUSE
OLD COUNTER FLASHING
APPLY ASPHALT
PRIMER ON MASONRY

8" STRIP OF
ROLL ROOFING
NAILED TO
OLD SHINGLES
PLUS ASPHALT
CEMENT

EMBED SHINGLES IN CEMENT

APPLY CEMENT OVER
SHINGLE ENDS & COVER
WITH STRIP OF ROLL
ROOFING

CHIMNEY FLASHING

Chimney flashing when reroofing can often make use of old counter-flashing when the old material is still serviceable.

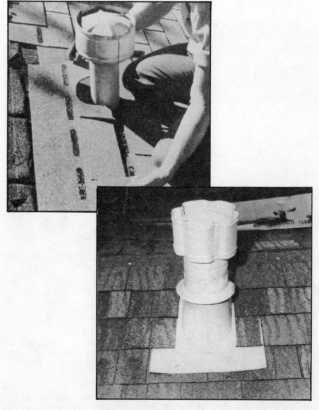

Two ways of flashing through roof projections such as plumbing stacks or ventilators. At far left, the technique when reroofing over an old roof, new shingles are cut to fit around the stack or vent and cemented down. In near left photo, where old roofing has been removed, the regular flashing flange interleaf with shingles is used as though it were a new construction job.

Aluminum foil-faced sealing tape can be a real time-saver in reroofing for flashing around plumbing and chimney roof projections. At left, the foil-faced sealer, which comes in rolls of varying widths, is pressed into place around the base of a plumbing pipe. At right, a 4-inch strip of the sealing material is pressed into position as base flashing

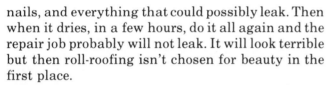

around a stone chimney. Called "Flashband," the material bonds to normal building materials. It is useful for other roof flashings also including such locations as side-wall junctions, antenna bases, skylights, and ventilators. Photos courtesy of Evode Inc.

nails, and everything that could possibly leak. Then when it dries, in a few hours, do it all again and the repair job probably will not leak. It will look terrible but then roll-roofing isn't chosen for beauty in the first place.

As for the scientific wonder roofing material—use tar, caulking, mastic, or epoxy, whatever gets the job done. If damage is severe, an attempt should be made to find a correct replacement material, but to be blunt most of the wonder-roof companies seem to go under at such a rate that finding them when you need a repair is almost impossible. They are doing wonderful things with plastic, of course, but the truth of the matter is that most of the materials coming out seem to break down over time. Sun, weather, and wind-driven sand and dirt seem to burn, bake, and slowly destroy the new materials. For that reason, it lasts a while and disappears. Getting some for replacement is largely a matter of luck.

In the end probably the most important thing to remember about roofs is that a roof that keeps out weather is a good roof. Most or all kinds of roofs can sustain massive amounts of seeming damage and still keep the weather out. Do not recover a roof just because a contractor going door to door comes by and points out how terrible your roof looks. If it is not letting weather through or leaking into the attic, causing very real problems, you need not worry; it

Cementing down both the flashing and the cut valley shingles, insures a tight valley that will drain well without leaking.

might last for several years before it becomes a truly necessary repair problem.

Do not let yourself be railroaded by contractors, even when the problem becomes blatant. When you have got pots and pans catching the drips coming through the ceiling still take the time to try repairing it yourself. You can do so without sustaining permanent damage to the house. If your try does not work, then call different contractors, get comparative bids, and make a calm choice.

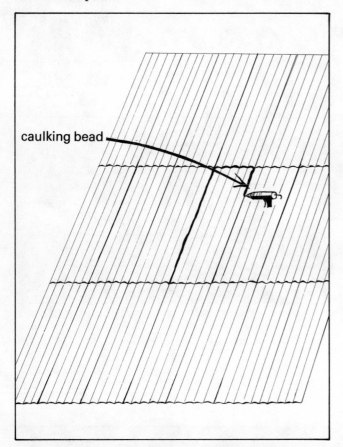

caulking bead

Metal roofing should always be handled with gloves, caulked liberally, nailed with special metal-roofing nails, and never repaired on rainy or windy days.

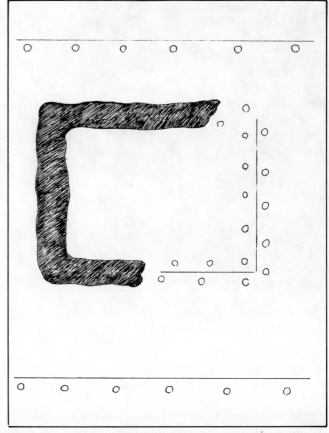

The most important item when repairing roll roofing is to tar the cut-seam liberally when done. Pack it in with a stick, working it wide and long, to make sure the area is leakproof.

Contractors

The premise of this book, as indicated by the title, is how to avoid calling in contractors. And in fully nine cases out of ten there is absolutely no need for calling them in; the homeowner can do the work on his own and do as good a job (often better) as that done by a contractor.

But now and then, for one reason or another, it is unavoidable. This is especially true for senior citizens who perhaps cannot go clambering around on a roof, or people not comfortable working with electrical problems.

For that reason a small chapter devoted to dealing with contractors—home repair contractors, to be specific—seems in order.

Perhaps because of the nature of repair work, since it is always a semiemergency or a problem that needs fixing now, home repair contractors seem to be particularly expensive.

There is no norm, of course, no set fee. Generally they charge what the traffic will bear. A job that might cost twenty dollars in one place could easily bring as much as a hundred and fifty in another area. It all depends on the demand and number of contractors in the area.

Be sure the materials and procedures specified for each bid are the same, so you will be able to compare accurately.

Because of that, and assuming there is time, shop around. Get several estimates on the repair job you are contemplating and take your time picking the one for the job.

Also, before selecting a repair contractor and after you get the estimate, ask for references. Then check the references. Check and verify everything before you hire and spend money for a job that might have disappointing results. But, if the job amounts to less than a hundred dollars, you are unlikely to be able to get bids. In this case it would be better to contact someone you know can be trusted to do the job well and will charge a fair (if not cheapest) price, without bids.

It perhaps goes without saying, but it might bear repeating—get everything in writing. Make the contractor detail the materials, with approximate prices for each, and labor costs, labor amounts, amount of time for the job, date started, and date he estimates completion.

Then check again. Call a few lumberyards and see if the material costs are fair, or even close. It is appalling, but some contractors have been known to double and even triple the amount paid for materials to pick up a few extra bucks. And actually, with material costs exploding upward, doubling a price can be a substantial amount of money.

Another trick tried by some of the more unscrupulous home repair contractors is to order much more material than needed to complete the job. They then take the surplus home and use it on the next job, passing the expense over to you in the meantime. With an itemized list, it is easy to check, and if he is buying four sheets of plywood to cover an area normally covered by one or getting three gallons of paint instead of one, drop him immediately.

As a final note, because sadly there is no way for knowing ahead of time, unless you personally know the contractor, what kind of work you will get, call the Better Business Bureau. They will not recommend one contractor over another, but they will tell you which ones to avoid.

The idea of being careful cannot be stressed too much. Literally millions of dollars annually are wasted on completely needless home repair work. Just in the area of heating systems alone, there are continual stories of teams of bunko artists going around, talking of vague dangers and unspeakable horrors, and selling new heating systems to the unsuspecting when nothing is needed. Some cities have special squads of police just for these crooked home repair contractors, and every fall these squads work steadily to quell the con games.

So be truly cautious if you have to hire a contractor to do the work. Treat the hiring as you would select a doctor; it may cost as much.

Spouts and Soffits

In a way, soffits are part of the roofing system, but they are also part of the roof-drain system and when the drains go bad they tend to wreck the soffits, where the drains are hooked on.

Drains and Spouts

A good maintenance system is critical in this area of the house. Clean drains, open gutters and downspouts with no leaves or branches fouling them up might mean, literally, ten or fifteen years in the life of the gutter and spout system.

To keep your downspouts from becoming overloaded, use the chart below as a guide for the size needed.

Roof area	Gutter diameter	Downspout diameter
Square feet	Inches	Inches
100-800	4	3
800-1,000	5	3
1,000-1,400	5	4
1,400-2,000	6	4

When maintenance falls down, so do the drains, and repair is an utter mess. Usually the old drain is nailed onto the last board of the soffit or eave and most often if the drain or gutter is rotted out enough to demand replacement, the board will also be ruined. Check it, and if it is bad take a crowbar and (working from a ladder) remove first the gutter and then the board, lifting the roofing material (which undoubtedly will not be rotted because it has got a longer life span than drains or wood) out of the way.

Wear long sleeves, goggles, a hard hat, and good gloves, and have a sturdy and secure ladder; then rip and tear. It will be unpleasant work but the sooner done the better.

Since the last board of the eave or soffit has been torn out, that is obviously the first item that needs repair. The best choice for replacement is a redwood board, because it resists rot; nail it back on the rafters with galvanized nails and then paint well with a good enamel and proper primers. The idea is to stop future rot before it can get started and before it can work back off the gutters. Anything that will help should be tried.

When the soffit board has been put back in place, painted, and allowed to dry, install the new gutter according to the instructions that come with the gutter. There are several different methods of installation, depending upon the type of gutter purchased, but they are all easy.

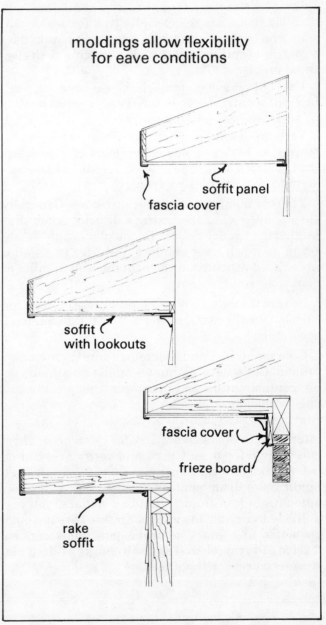

Aluminum products are also available: this drawing indicates varying eave conditions handled by different moldings. These are only a few of the several variations possible. Art courtesy of Alcan Building Products

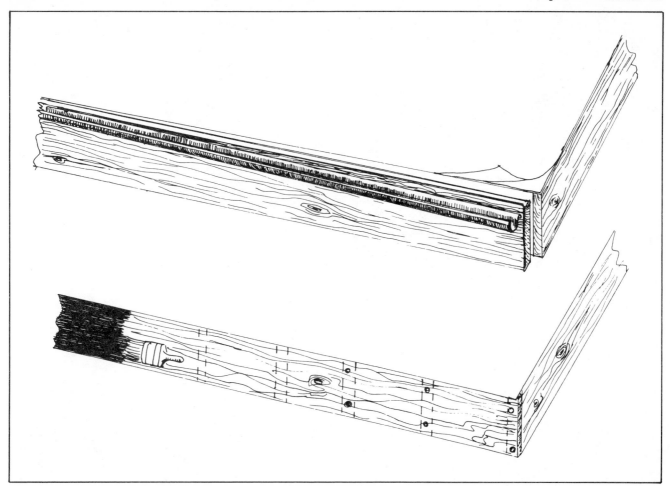

After working the gutter off and then the last soffit board, lift back the roof material and replace old soffit board with a new one—preferably redwood. Nail with galvanized nails; prime; use oil-based enamel paint. Re-nail gutter to new soffit, or replace with new gutter or trough.

A couple of helpful hints from the past might also help you. First, people used to paint their gutters with a good coat of plain roofing tar. It is a mess to do but once the gutter is in place nobody can see it, and it does offer another coat of very inexpensive protection. Second, in many areas of the country, water shortages have been critical. If you have some old barrels—this is how they used to get soft water for washing hair—you might wish to store the rainwater for irrigation purposes. Just put the barrel under the spout; it is amazing how fast it will fill.

If the spouts rot they have to be replaced. This amounts to pulling and replacing brackets.

If your downspouts become plugged with leaves, first try using a hose. From the top just feed a hose going full blast down into the spout, and keep poking until it works through.

If the hose does not work—it may not if a squirrel has decided to use the spout for winter storage—rent or borrow a plumber's snake and work it up from the bottom while feeding the hose down from the top. Nothing can withstand the two forces working

This galvanized steel gutter was painted before adequate weathering could remove processing chemicals. The only lasting cure is a new gutter.

Aluminum soffits may offer the simplest route to a complete soffit renovation. Panels must be cut to proper length and slid into position engaging the edge of the previously applied panel. Note that the homeowner is handling panels by edges to avoid fingermarks on the surfaces.

Fasten panels to the old soffit material—a small Bostitch Pneumatic stapler can cut time. The stapler has a slightly projecting nozzle to allow stapling in panel grooves without touching the panel faces.

Staples are driven through soffit panels into the edge of old fascia board.

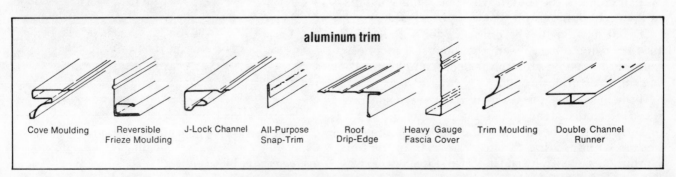

aluminum trim

Cove Moulding | Reversible Frieze Moulding | J-Lock Channel | All-Purpose Snap-Trim | Roof Drip-Edge | Heavy Gauge Fascia Cover | Trim Moulding | Double Channel Runner

Soffit panels are carried up to the diagonal J-channel and marked for 45-degree angle cuts. Then panel sections are slid into place with end cuts nestling into the J-channel.

Soffit corners can be handled with a length of double-back-to-back J-channel, stapled into place at a 45-degree angle on a building corner. The doubled J-channel is cut slightly long to allow for mitering cuts, (using aviation-type tinsnips) at each end.

Here is a front view of soffit installation just before the fascia cover is installed, which will conceal the open ends of the soffit panels. Along this brick wall narrow frieze board has been capped with a custom brake-bent aluminum strip.

together. Move quickly aside when everything lets go.

Water draining from a spout often brings an erosion problem which could eventually destroy your yard.

Cement pads are available to put under the drains just for such purposes. Or if you would rather make your own, it is very simple. Get a sack of premix cement for each pad you want, make a wooden frame 10 x 24 inches out of 1 x 4 lumber, and fill it with slightly wet cement. Then, wearing rubber gloves, "sculpt" a water pocket and groove down the middle with your hands and let it cure for a couple of days before putting it in place. (See the illustration.) A sheet of galvanized steel will also work.

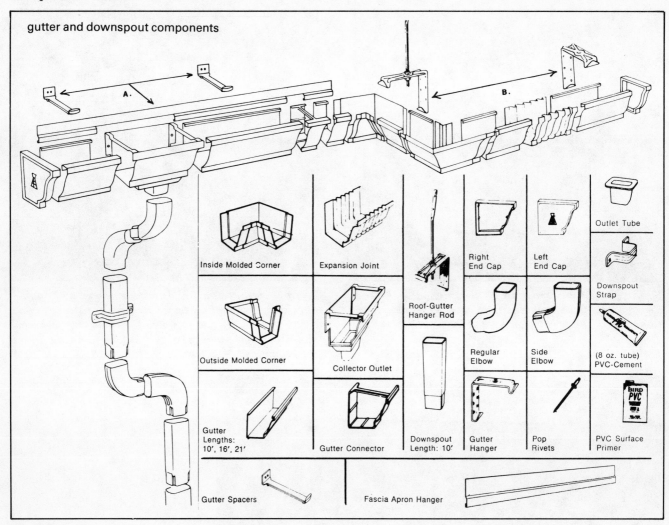

gutter and downspout components

Inside Molded Corner

Expansion Joint

Roof-Gutter Hanger Rod

Right End Cap

Left End Cap

Outlet Tube

Outside Molded Corner

Collector Outlet

Regular Elbow

Side Elbow

Downspout Strap

(8 oz. tube) PVC-Cement

Gutter Lengths: 10', 16', 21'

Gutter Connector

Downspout Length: 10'

Gutter Hanger

Pop Rivets

PVC Surface Primer

Gutter Spacers

Fascia Apron Hanger

Components of a solid vinyl downspout system; this brand is produced in white and does not require additional painting. Two methods of hanging are indicated as "A" and "B." Art courtesy of Bird & Son

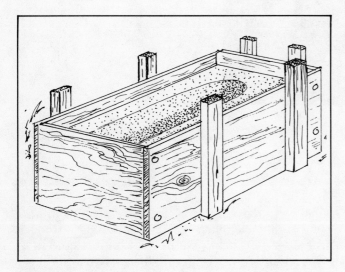

Making your own cement pad to prevent erosion is not hard: build forms for concrete and sculpt a water pocket; be sure to let concrete cure before placing pad beneath water spout.

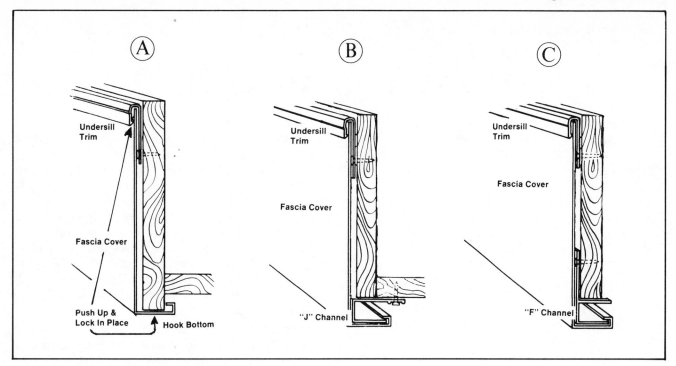

Soffit boards can be replaced with kits: one such is a vinyl fascia-soffit combination that can be adapted to different eave conditions. (A) Only the fascia surface is recovered, not the soffit. (B) J-channels are used at the eave and at the house wall, fastened to an existing soffit. New panels are installed below. (C) Use is made of an F-channel at eave and the house wall where there was no existing soffit material. New soffit panels in this case are held in place by the channels alone. Art courtesy of Bird & Son

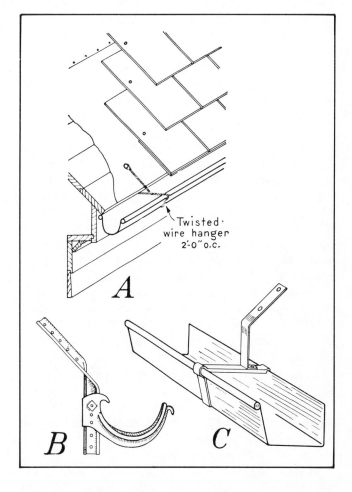

Hanging eaves troughs are a cheaper alternative to built-in gutter downspouts: (A) half-round type; (B) adjustable hanger; (C) box type.

Concrete Surfaces

All materials deteriorate over time, and concrete is very susceptible. Accidents and wear-and-tear often leave their mark on concrete; freshly cast concrete can be damaged when forms are removed; and, cracks are a common problem.

There are several kinds of repair materials and techniques. The emphasis here will be on those which can be easily handled by the homeowner without special tools or equipment.

Identifying the Problem

Here are some definitions of terms to help you recognize the more common types of concrete damage or deterioration.

Cracks In most cases, cracks should be considered "active," that is, they continue to develop. An unstable subbase can result in uneven settlement and cracking. Incorrect jointing to handle temperature-change effects also results in active cracks.

A "dormant" crack means that it was caused by a factor not expected to reoccur, such as temporary overloading—for example, a car or truck driving over a slab that had not been built for that kind of a load.

Crazing Crazing cracks are shallow cracks that form a hexagonal pattern. These cracks usually occur shortly after the concrete has hardened. Crazing can be caused by the concrete slab drying out too rapidly—by a rapid loss of moisture from the surface of fresh concrete or by the concrete being placed on a dry subgrade. Other causes could be: too much water in the mix, or excessive finishing. Crazing cracks are usually dormant.

Dusting Dusting occurs when the surface of the concrete becomes soft and rubs off readily under traffic. Common causes of dusting include: too wet concrete mixes, excessive finishing, or inadequate curing.

Efflorescence Efflorescence is the appearance of crystalline salts on a concrete surface. This is caused by water that migrates from the interior of the concrete to the surface; or, as the water evaporates, salts are deposited. It does not hurt the concrete, but mars its appearance.

Holes Whether large or small, if a hole is not cleaned and shaped properly before patching, the patch will probably not hold. It is important to repair holes as soon as possible. Sometimes a "hole" is caused when concrete sticks to the form as it is being stripped (removed). This usually occurs when the forms were not properly coated with oil before concreting. Small holes, called bugholes, may occur along the surface next to a form and are due primarily to entrapped air bubbles. Honeycombing is another so-called hole, but of a different nature. Honeycombing results from the coarse aggregate being placed with an insufficient amount of mortar, because the mix is undersanded, or because poor placing techniques are followed. To repair these areas you must force mortar into the voids, or remove all loose and poorly bonded material and then replace it all with concrete.

Popouts Popouts, shallow surface holes, usually occur in slabs. They are caused by expansion of a particle near the concrete surface. Wet or frozen shales, cherts, lignites, and limestones are likely to cause popouts. Some absorbent aggregates that expand when exposed to freezing also cause popouts.

Scaling Scaling is the sloughing off of thin surface layers of concrete. Scaling can be caused by freezing and thawing of the concrete, use of deicing salts on concrete which is not air-entrained, poor finishing practices, repeated wetting and drying of the concrete, or chemical attack on the concrete.

Spalling Spalling is a loosely used term; it usually refers to chunks of concrete that have been broken from the surface by mechanical damage or impact. Spalling is also caused by corrosion of the reinforcing steel.

Repairs

Most manufacturers furnish specific instructions on the use of their repair products. Be sure to read and to follow them. Listed below are some basic techniques.

Acid etching. Safety precautions must be followed when working with acids. Most acids used for etching concrete cause burns when they come in contact with the skin, and some acids also give off noxious fumes. You should wear protective clothing, gloves, boots, and safety goggles.

Efflorescence can be removed with a 10 percent solution of hydrochloric acid. Sometimes acid etching is used to remove a material from the surface that might impair the bond of a patching material. Usually the concrete is brushed vigorously with a stiff broom with the acid solution. After etching, the acid solution should be thoroughly flushed from the surface as soon as it has ceased foaming.

CONCRETE DAMAGE:
Repair Techniques and Repair Materials

Concrete Damage	Repair Technique	Repair Materials
Active cracks	Caulking	Elastic sealants
Dormant cracks	Caulking	Bituminous coatings
	Coatings	Elastic sealants
	Concrete replacement	Epoxies
		Expanding mortars
		High-speed setting materials
		Latex-modified concrete
		Portland cement concrete and mortar
Crazing	Coatings	Epoxies
		Latex-modified concrete
		Linseed oil
		Portland cement mortar
Dusting	Acid etching	Epoxies
	Coatings	Latex-modified concrete
		Linseed oil
		Surface hardeners
Efflorescence	Acid etching	Portland cement mortar
Small holes	Coatings	Dry pack
	Mortar replacement	Epoxies
		High-speed setting materials
		Latex-modified concrete
		Portland cement mortar
Large holes	Coatings	Epoxies
	Concrete replacement	Expanding mortars
		High-speed setting materials
		Latex-modified concrete
		Portland cement concrete and mortar
Popouts	Coatings	Bituminous coatings
		Epoxies
		Latex-modified concrete
Scaling	Coatings	Epoxies
		Latex-modified concrete
		Linseed oil

Adapted from "Concrete Repair Problems: Causes and Cures," *Concrete Construction,* November, 1969.

Caulking Caulking involves filling fairly narrow openings (cracks) with a plastic compound. Cracks can often be sealed with an elastomeric caulking material.

Coatings Coatings are materials of liquid or plastic consistency that can be applied directly over concrete. Some coating materials are epoxy resins, bituminous compounds, linseed oil, and silicone preparations.

Concrete replacement Sometimes conditions are so bad that only complete removal and replacement of the damaged concrete will solve the problem.

Mortar replacement Mortar replacement is usually confined to shallow holes. The following steps should be followed to achieve a successful repair:

- Thoroughly clean and shape the cavity
- Obtain a good bond between mortar and the old concrete
- Vary the consistency of the mortar depending on whether the hole is in a floor or wall

- Eliminate or reduce shrinkage
- Cure thoroughly

Sack-rubbing Sack-rubbing will often improve the appearance of a concrete surface with stains or small bugholes. First spray the concrete with water. Then rub damp mortar over the surface and into the voids with a rubber float or a piece of burlap. Add enough white cement to the mortar to match the color of the surrounding concrete. And, of course, cure the concrete as usual.

A sand finish can be achieved the same way, except that you would rub a creamy, rather than a stiff, mortar over the surface.

Sack-rubbing is most effective when done shortly after forms are stripped. Any large voids should be repaired before sack-rubbing.

Many products are available. In all cases, follow the manufacturer's instructions.

For cases where you need water resistance, use a bituminous coating. It can be applied in a thin coat, and is often used to waterproof the exteriors of basement walls.

There are also epoxy-based compounds for many types of concrete repairs. They harden rapidly and resist water. Epoxies can be mixed with fine aggregates to reduce unit cost and make the repair material go further. Epoxy-based compounds are useful where an adhesive is needed to bond plastic concrete to hardened concrete or to bond rigid materials to each other; for patching; or when a thin, strong coating is needed over concrete.

Another popular product is a type of expanding mortar. This was developed to overcome or minimize shrinking, and can be especially useful in patching.

If you want a speedy set, there are high-speed setting materials that harden and develop strength in a matter of minutes. They come either as admixtures to be added to the mortar or concrete, or as ready-to-use materials requiring only the addition of water.

Linseed oil is used when scaling has occurred but without severe damage to warrant more extensive repair. The usual solution is a mixture of 50 percent linseed oil and 50 percent mineral or petroleum spirits (by volume). Linseed oil is particularly effective in protecting new concrete when applied before the first freeze and prior to the application of deicing salt. It penetrates the surface of the concrete to a depth of about ⅛ inch. The oil inhibits further damage by forming a film that water and salt solutions do not readily penetrate.

Patching

Preparing the surface to be patched Whatever material is used to repair a damaged concrete surface, the patch will only be as strong as the surface to which it is bonded. Make sure the surface is clean and sound. It must not be contaminated with oil, grease, paint, or mud. The surface can be scrubbed clean with a water-soluble detergent. Heavy deposits of material should be scraped off before scrubbing. Also, there is no point patching over unsound material. Any scaling, crumbling, or loose material must be removed down to clean, hard concrete. Hand picks or chisels can be used to remove unsound material. The depth to which material should be removed from a damaged area will depend on the patching technique and patching compound chosen. If you use portland cement concrete or mortar, the area to be repaired should be removed to a depth of at least 1½ inches. If using a latex-modified mortar, the cut can be less since this compound works well for thinner patches.

Portland cement patches When using portland cement concrete or mortar as the patching material, the first step is to soak the cleaned bonding surface with water for at least an hour, and preferably overnight, before patching begins.

If the patch is being made in new concrete, work should begin just as soon as possible after removing (stripping) the forms or molds. If the patch is in old concrete, you want to wait after soaking until all surface water has disappeared. The old concrete, just prior to placing the patching mix, should be damp but still slightly absorbent.

Next, a bonding layer is applied to the clean, damp surface. On horizontal surfaces use a grout of

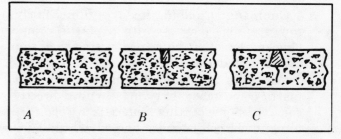

The right and wrong method for patching a small shallow hole in a concrete wall or slab. (A) Wrong—This patch is too shallow. The featheredge will soon chip out, and this patch will not hold. (B) Right—The edges should be vertical. The patch is deep enough for a good body of mortar to be placed; this patch will stay.

Repairing a wide crack (A), about 1/16 inch or wider. There are two good ways to cut out the crack for patching: (B) a vertical cut for the edges or (C) an undercut.

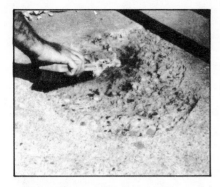  

The steps in repairing a damaged concrete slab. Top row (left to right): Preparing the surface by cleaning out all loose debris. Priming the surface. Next, a grout coating is placed. The grout of portland cement and water should have the consistency of thick paint. Bottom row (left to right): Placing and spreading mortar should follow immediately. Finishing the patch with a trowel. Repair completed. Photos courtesy of Concrete Construction Publications Inc.

portland cement and water mixed to the consistency of thick paint; it should be forced into the base by firm brushing with a semistiff bristled brush. On vertical surfaces the bonding layer should be composed of 1 part portland cement and 1 part sand. This mortar should be mixed ½ to 3 hours before use and should be of plastering consistency when applied. Occasional mixing during this period will keep the mortar from stiffening, but do not retemper with water. The bonding layer should be applied to a thickness of about ¼ inch using a stucco brush, but do not apply it too far in advance of the main repair. Otherwise the bonding mortar will dry out.

In general, the mortar or concrete used in the patch should be of the same materials and in the same proportions as that of the base concrete. Since a patch tends to be darker than the surrounding concrete, it is a good idea to substitute white cement for a part of the ordinary gray portland cement used.

For repairing the normal shallow spall, the patching mortar should be built up in layers about ⅜ inches thick. Keep each layer moist for a day or two before placing the next, cross-scratching it to provide a good bonding surface for the next layer. If the patch to be filled is deep, it is often more practical to

build a form over the area and to pack concrete behind it.

The patching mix should contain just enough water to give the mix an earth-dry consistency, so that when a pat of mix is squeezed it will "cake," just leaving a trace of moisture in the palm.

On horizontal surfaces, patching concrete should be vigorously hand-tamped in place. On vertical surfaces the concrete should be carefully rodded into place, making sure that the concrete is well compacted and fills corners fully. Then trowel or float the surfaces to the desired finish.

The patch must be thoroughly cured. The patched area should be kept constantly moist for several days and, if practical, curing should continue for as long as a week. If the patch is not carefully cured, it may dry out and shrink away from the old surface.

Epoxy bonding agents Patching with an epoxy-based adhesive is likely to achieve a better bond than patching using a portland cement mortar coating.

When using epoxy adhesives, follow the manufacturer's instructions. The epoxy materials usually come in the form of a two-component system—the base resin and a hardener. Once the two are mixed the curing process begins with a highly reactive chemical process.

a. Cut out all disintegrated concrete until a solid surface is reached.

b. Brush out all loose concrete, chips, and dirt. Dampen area with clean water.

c. While area is still damp, apply a grout coat of patching compound. Work the grout well into the area to be patched.

d. Mix patching compound to a mortar consistency.

e. Force the patching mortar into the area to be repaired, in layers not exceeding 1 inch.

f. Scratch first layer while material is still soft, to assist in maintaining bond between layers.

Steps in repairing a broken concrete corner—applicable to steps and curbs—with a prepared patching mortar, Thorite.

The quantity of bonding agent to be mixed at one time should not be more than can be used up within the pot-life of the agent. This period will be noted by the manufacturer, but generally the pot life is about 2 or 3 hours. Pot life means the period during which application is possible. Most bonding agents remain tacky for 1-2 hours after the specified pot life. The new concrete for a patch should be placed anytime during this tacky stage. Tacky set usually begins about ½ hour after application of the epoxy agent, when the free solvents in the mixture have evaporated.

The epoxy bonding material is best applied by stiff bristle brush; this method fills all angles and pores of the surface. Then the stiff mortar is placed and finished.

Be careful when using epoxies; make sure there is adequate ventilation since vapors can irritate the eyes, throat, and lungs. Also important, keep the materials off the skin since this may lead to severe rashes; always wear gloves. If you spill resin on the skin, wash it off immediately with lots of ordinary soap and water. Do not use a solvent; it will only cause greater skin penetration.

Crack repair Crack repair depends on how large the crack is, its size and depth, and whether it is an active or dormant crack.

If the crack is active, an elastic sealer or caulking material is the best way to seal the crack and still allow movement.

The dormant crack can be filled permanently with a patching mortar or compound: portland cement mortar, epoxy mortar, or a latex-modified mortar. For a hairline crack, sometimes a grout made of portland cement and water is sufficient. Mix the grout to a thick paste consistency. Force the paste into the crack with a trowel or putty knife, and

g. Apply next layer of patching mortar.

h. Overfill the area so that the patch is slightly larger than the surrounding area.

i. Shave off excess until patch conforms to the adjacent area.

j. The patch has been completed and repainted. Photos by Standard Dry Wall Products

then smooth level with the concrete surface. As in all repairs, the crack must be cleaned before filling, and the surface should be dampened prior to using the portland cement grout. This kind of patch should be moist cured.

If the crack is more than 1/16 inch wide it should be chipped away and widened with a hardened-steel chisel. To hold the patching material, the sides of the cut should either be straight or undercut. For small repairs, a prepackaged mortar mix is ideal. These come in packages as small as 5 pounds. A latex-modified mortar or epoxy mortar works extremely well in these situations. If you use a straight portland cement mortar, a typical mix would be 1 part cement to 3 parts sand. Follow the manufacturer's instructions in application. Most repairs call for the old concrete to be well soaked with water and damp at the surface when the mortar patch is applied, and it does not hurt at all to soak the repair area overnight. Once the area has been cleaned thoroughly, force the patching material into the crack, then smooth, and cure.

Repairing steps and curbs Damaged steps and sidewalks are dangerous as well as ugly. Broken corners can be patched with portland cement mortar, but some of today's ready-to-use patching mortars are even easier.

The broken corner should be chiseled and cleaned out. Undercut the edges. Simple formwork may be required to hold the patch if the area is large. At other times the stiff patching mortar will support itself. The patch is tamped and compacted, then floated and troweled. Portland cement mortar requires curing—keep the concrete damp—as do some of the compounds. Wet burlap is a good curing method.

By the way, if the broken corner or piece is still in good shape, it is possible to glue it back in place. Clean the area and use an epoxy or latex mortar (some products are premixed, some you will have to mix). Butter the broken piece with the patching mortar and hold or brace it in place, usually 10 to 15 minutes. After the mortar has stiffened, the excess that has squeezed out can be cleaned off with a trowel or putty knife.

Concrete Stains

Staining may be natural causes or manmade: water run-off can deposit soot or dissolved mineral salts; the family automobile may leak oil on a garage floor. Or someone spills a can of paint. Fortunately you do not have to be either a chemist or a magician to remove most stains. Almost any stain can be removed from concrete; old, long-neglected stains may require repeated treatments.

To preface a description of specific treatments, here is some general advice on procedures and precautions. The materials and chemicals mentioned below are readily available at drugstores, chemical or laundry supply houses, and possibly at paint or building supply centers. Under normal circumstances the cleaning materials can be used both indoors and outdoors without danger. Naturally, two very basic elementary safety precautions should be taken (a) wash hands thoroughly after use, and (b) maintain adequate ventilation.

After the stain has been removed it is good practice to wash the area thoroughly with clean water to remove any residue particles of filler, and to be certain that no soluble and possibly detrimental salts remain on the concrete.

If you are not exactly sure what the stain is, it sometimes is better to test a cleaning treatment. Improper materials or techniques could result in spreading a stain over a larger area than originally involved. The best method is to prepare a small trial quantity of the cleaning agent and to apply it at the most inconspicuous point to assess its value. The composition or strength can then be varied appropriately. This trial-and-error approach applies particularly to the fillers used to form a paste. Different fillers have varying abilities to cling to vertical surfaces.

Also remember that on old concrete, accumulated dirt also disappears with the stains. A limited clean area in a sea of darkened concrete may, in effect, seem just like another stain. Time, wear, and weathering should solve this problem, so that the spot will blend in with the rest of the concrete.

Treatments Rust stains on concrete are common. They usually result from weathering of steel or iron attached to or resting on the concrete.

The cleaning materials needed are: sodium citrate crystals, crystals of sodium hydrosulfite, and a paste of whiting and water.

The surface should be soaked with a solution made of 1 part sodium citrate crystals in 6 parts of water. Dip white cloth in this solution and paste it over the stain for 10 to 15 minutes. Or, apply the solution by brush at 5-to 10-minute intervals until the area is thoroughly soaked.

On horizontal surfaces you can sprinkle a thin layer of sodium hydrosulfite crystals, moisten with water, and cover it with a paste of whiting and water.

On vertical surfaces: soak with the sodium citrate solution, place the paste of whiting on a trowel, sprinkle it with sodium hydrosulfite crystals, and plaster the paste over the stained area—making sure the crystals are in contact with the stained area.

Allow the paste to soak in for at least 10 to 20 minutes. Do not leave the paste in place more than one hour, as black staining may result. Remove and flush with clear water. If stain remains, repeat the treatment, but usually a single application is adequate.

Aluminum stains Aluminum stains usually show up as white deposits on the concrete. The cleaning agent required is a 10 to 20 percent muriatic acid solution. (Remember to observe the label precautions, since muriatic acid can affect eyes, skin and breathing.)

The white deposit may be removed by scrubbing. On colored concrete, weaker solutions should be used. Flush with clear water after removal to prevent etching.

Grease stains Grease will normally not penetrate very far into good dense concrete. Scrape off all excess grease from the surface and scrub with scouring powder, soap, trisodium phosphate, or detergent.

If staining persists, try a solvent. Avoid using free solvents such as gasoline or kerosene, since these only increase the degree of penetration.

Make a paste using a solvent and inert powdered filler. The solvent can be benzene, refined naptha solvent, or a chlorinated hydrocarbon solvent such as trichloroethylene. The filler can be hydrated lime, whiting, or talc. Apply the paste to the stain and do not remove until the paste is thoroughly dry. Repeat the application as often as necessary. Then scrub with strong soap, scouring powder, trisodium phosphate, or detergent (some are specially formulated for use on concrete). Rinse with clear water at end of treatment.

Oil stains Lubricating or petroleum oil readily penetrates into the concrete surface. With any oil spillage there will be little danger of staining if the free oil is removed promptly. It should be soaked up immediately with an absorbent material such as paper towels or cloth. Wiping should be avoided, as it spreads the stains and drives the oil into the concrete.

Cover the spot with a dry, powdered, absorbent inert material (hydrated lime, whiting, powdered talc or portland cement). Leave it for one day. Repeat this treatment until no more oil is absorbed by the powder. If a stain persists or if oil has been allowed to remain for some time and has penetrated the concrete, other materials will be necessary.

Oils that have solidified should be scraped off as much as possible. Then scrub the area with a clean strong soap, scouring powder, trisodium phosphate or proprietary detergents specially formulated for use on concrete. By the way, a water softener from the laundry room—Calgon—works extremely well. Wet down the concrete surface and sprinkle on the Calgon (or similar material). Let stand for a little while. Then scrub and flush with water. This will remove most of the free oil. The following treatments can also be used (they are somewhat similar):

1. Make a paste of a suitable solvent, such as benzol, and an inert powdered filler (hydrated lime, whiting or talc). Apply the paste to the area and allow it to remain in position for at least 1 hour after all solvent has evaporated. Remove and scrub with clear water. Repeat as necessary.
2. Make a poultice with a solution of 5 percent sodium hydroxide (caustic soda). Let dry for 20 to 24 hours, remove, and scrub the surface with clear water. Repeat as necessary.

Paint stains Dried paint films can be removed satisfactorily by most commercial paint removers. Probably the most effective paint removers are based on methylene dichloride, and are available as liquids, gels, or pastes. Do not use paint strippers that contain acetic acid; these will remove the paint, but may also damage the concrete surface.

The remover should be applied liberally to the area and allowed to penetrate the film for 20 to 30 minutes. Gentle scrubbing will then loosen the paint film and allow it to be peeled or washed off. Wash with water. Any remaining residue can be scrubbed off with scouring powder. Color that has penetrated the surface can be washed out with dilute hydrochloride or phosphoric acid.

This treatment can be applied also to dried enamel, lacquer, or linseed-oil-based varnish. For shellac stains, the paint remover is replaced by alcohol.

Paint removers should be used on freshly spilled paint or on films less than three days old, since they only tend to increase penetration of the fresh paint into the surface. Absorption with soft cloth or paper towels, followed by vigorous scrubbing, is recommended.

Coffee stains Coffee stains can be removed by applying cloth saturated in glycerin diluted with four times its volume of water.

Soot Soot and smoke can be removed by scrubbing the area with ordinary scouring powder. This is followed by an application of sodium hypochlorite (ordinary bleach).

Glossary

Appliances Washers, driers, etc.

Asphalt tile Square tiles for flooring.

Baseboard units Baseboard heating units, either electric or hot water.

Bearings (furnace) The roller bearings in a blower on the heater, or in a pump on a hot water heating system.

Blower fan The heat-moving, or air-moving part of a forced air heating system, the rotating fan.

Boiler The water-heating part (tank) of a hot water or steam heating system.

Box beam A two-by-four and plywood beam structure which allows great strength with light, or comparatively light woods; the plywood is nailed to the sides of the beam, "boxing" it in.

Breaker (circuit) Protective switch, in a panel (often in a closet) which "pops" and opens an overloaded circuit.

Butt, shingle The heavy, or thick, or bottom end of a shingle.

Canted boards "Tipped" or slanted floor boards.

Carbide blades Carbide (hard metal) tipped saw blades for a circular saw—very tough.

Casing The "sleeve" of the inside of the well hole going down into the ground—usually metal.

Catalyst Chemical activator for epoxy or fiberglass resin or putty.

Caulking compound Putty-like mixture, which comes in a tube usually of plastic base, used to plug or "caulk" holes.

Caulking gun Small gun-like applicator for using caulking compound tubes.

Ceramic tiles Hard, ceramic-clay tiles usually used in baths or kitchens.

Circuit Electrical term meaning the flow to and from an electrical device—often used to mean wiring.

Circuit breaker See Breaker.

Collar nut An outside tightening nut, out and around another piece of pipe.

Color coded Term used in electrical application; wires are color coded (black is power, white is neutral, green is ground) to prevent mistakes.

Composition tiles Asphalt or vinyl floor tiles.

Construction adhesive Special glue, which comes in the same tubes as caulking compound, for gluing large areas inexpensively.

Corner brackets L-shaped brackets for tightening the corners of doors, especially wooden screen doors.

Countersinking screws To use a cone-shaped drill bit to make a sunken cone to take the head of a countersunk screw.

Coupling Small section of pipe which slides over two ends of pipe or is threaded to take them and (with galvanized) to hold them together.

Cover plate The plastic plate over outlets and switches.

Crystal Inexpensive version of plate-like glass; has slight "ripple" effect.

Drain tube Water pipe (plastic or metal) which is meant to drain a pressure water area (around footings, as an example).

Dry rot Actually a form of mildew, very advanced which rots wood in attics.

Drywall knife Wide application "knife," not sharp, that looks like a large putty knife, for working drywall mud.

Drywall mud Spackling mud, or drywall cement (either premixed or powder) for repairing drywall.

Drywall tape Paper tape used to cover the seams between sheets of drywall—does not have an adhesive back.

Ducts The metal piping (sheetmetal) system for moving hot air around in a hot air heating system.

Eaves Edge of the roof parallel with the ground.

Emery cloth Cloth-backed sandpaper.

Enamel Oil based paint, usually used outside or in high moisture areas (kitchen, bath),

Epoxy Extremely strong, plastic-based adhesive which must be mixed prior to using.

Feathering Working the edge of a repair, either paint or drywall mud, back into the existing finish.

Fiberglass insulation Insulating material of fiberglass, with paper and/or tinfoil backing, which goes between studs or in rafters.

Fiberglass putty A pre-thickened filler made of shredded fiberglass and epoxy resin.

Filter Air cleaning filter in a hot air—forced air—heating system.

Flame chamber Portion of heating system which holds the actual gas flame.

Flat trowel Rectangular metal trowel used for working wide areas of mud (drywall) or cement.

Floor joist Edge-up board beneath floor which supports the flooring.

Flux Chemical (acid) cleaning material used in soldering.

Fuse Small, screw-in container with a wire that melts and opens the circuit if overloaded; usually found in older homes.

Fuse box Panel (usually in closet) which holds all the protective fuses for the different circuits in the house.

Galvanized nails Nails coated with zinc to stop rusting.

Galvanized pipe Plumbing pipe, usually found in older homes, which has been coated with zinc to retard rust and/or corrosion.

Gate valve Faucet handle type valve, like the kind on the side of a house for a hose.

Glass cutter Small tool, with a tiny, hard cutting wheel, for cutting glass.

Glazing compound Putty, for windows, now sometimes made of a plastic base material.

Glazing points Small metal points which push into a wooden window frame to hold the glass in place before puttying.

Graphite lube Powdered graphite, in a small tube, used for dry-lubrication.

Grout Filler material, usually dryish mixture of cement, used for filling open cracks and gaps, most often in foundation.

Gutters Half-pipes along the eaves to channel the water off the roof.

Guy wires Wire cables or wires used for support, as in supporting a television antenna on the roof.

Gym-seal Varnish-like, *hard* finish for gloss wooden floors, as in typical basketball gyms.

Hand drywall saw Small, single-blade, keyhole type saw for cutting drywall; has very stiff blade and coarse teeth.

Handsaw Non-electric saw for cutting wood.

Heat-sensing switch Circuit breaker (or) thermostat.

Heater housing (baseboard) The metal housing, sheet metal in construction, around the radiating elements in a baseboard heater.

Hot water system Heating system which circulates hot water through pipes to distribute heat.

Jack Device to lift heavy loads.

Jack, roof Device for holding scaffold up on a roof.

Joint cement See *drywall mud.*

Lap siding Exterior house siding made of boards which overlap.

Latch assemblies Door-latching mechanisms.

Latex base paint A water base paint, for interior use, dries flat.

Lath and plaster Old method of covering interior walls; found in older homes.

Line surge A surge of power, more common now than in the past due to energy problems, which causes the voltage in a house to increase slightly.

Linseed oil A wood-treatment oil made from flax.

Locksets Door latch assemblies.

Metal siding A house siding, made of sheet aluminum (most often), used in place of lap siding.

Mitered boards Boards cut on a mitered (45°) angle.

Nail punch Tapered punch for setting finishing nails.

Nonfilling wood rasp Wood rasp with holes through the rasp surface so it won't fill.

Outlet Wall electrical outlet.

Overload Too many appliances or tools on one circuit.

Packing Material inside faucet housing that keeps the housing from seep-leaking.

Paint scraper Bladed device for scraping off old paint.

Pilot hole Small hole drilled first to allow a bigger bit to be used.

Pipe rot Rust-rot of galvanized or metal plumbing pipes, usually found in older homes.

Pipe wrench Wrench with backward-sloping teeth to turn smooth pipe.

Plastic base paints See *latex base paints.*

Plywood siding Exterior siding, made of sheet plywood, but often made to look like other forms of siding.

Pressed board Another name for particleboard, a floor sheeting.

Pressure switching system The switching system on a well pressure tank, which turns the pump on and off.

Pressure tank That portion of a well system, a kind of reservoir, which holds the reserve of water for switching purposes.

Primer Base paint, undercoating before regular paint on "raw" surfaces.

Propane torch (also butane torch) A small tank-fed propane torch for soldering and other light heat applications.

P.S.I. Pounds per square inch.

Putty See *glazing compound.*

Radiation fins Small fins on a hot water heating system which radiate the heat; hidden under the baseboard units.

Rafters Roof support system.

Reset switch Mini-circuit breaker located on the appliance or pump; usually a red button.

Ring washer Large washer.

Roll roofing Composition asphalt roofing in roll form; wide bands of roofing.

Roofing nails Big-headed, short, galvanized nails for roof application.

Rotary saw Electric handsaw with circular blade.

Saber saw Electrical, hand-held saw which has an up and down motion of the blade.

Septic system Sewage disposal system for the single home.

Sheetrock Drywall.

Shopknife Small all-around knife with very sharp blade.

Sill plate Board that runs around the foundation on which the house sits.

Soffit Underside of the eaves.

Spackling paste Drywall mud.

Stapler Heavy stapler, gun type, not desk type.

Subfloor Plywood flooring beneath floor surface.

Sump-pump A small pump lowered into shallow water (used most often in basements) to drain it.

Tar Roofing mastic, a plastic-based tar-like substance.

Tile field The portion of a septic system, a field of porous rocks covered with earth, that spreads the waste liquid out and allows it to sink and purify.

Torque Winding energy, associated with a wrench.

Tracks (sliding door) Metal tracks above and below a sliding door.

Trowel Tool for working cement, most often spade-shaped.

Vinyl sheeting Imitation wood siding, sometimes in lap form, sometimes panel.

Volts Unit of electrical work energy, as in 110 volts or 220 volts.

Index